PROFILES IN
COURAGEOUS
MANHOOD

by

Edwin Louis Cole

ALBURY PUBLISHING
Tulsa, Oklahoma

Profiles in Courageous Manhood
ISBN 1-57778-087-6
Copyright © 1998 by Edwin Louis Cole
Christian Men's Network
International Communication Center
P. O. Box 10
Grapevine, Texas 76099-0010
USA

Published by ALBURY PUBLISHING
P. O. Box 470406
Tulsa, Oklahoma 74147-0406

TABLE OF CONTENTS

INTRODUCTION:

WHAT IS A
COURAGEOUS MAN?

Heroes are men who act in a moment of time on a need greater than themselves — whether Old Testament prophets, athletes in today's sports, or just ordinary men in the everyday course of life. In the Bible they call them "patriarchs." In sports they call them "stars." In our world of negativity and compromise, those who achieve positive victories are called simply "uncommon men" — courageous men who shine like stars in the darkest night. They become the patriarchs of faith for their families, friends, churches, and even communities.

Like stars, they also are sometimes obscured by clouds of controversy, the fog of ignorance, someone "raining on their parade," or just plain old humility. But I know such men, and they are uncommon men in my estimation.

Men need courage for five reasons: To hold convictions, to change, to admit need, to face reality, and to make decisions.[1] The men on the following pages exemplify such courage.

A marked characteristic in every one is a love of truth. One reason they love truth is because each has a love of Him Who is Truth. Openly, unashamedly, in boldness, they declare their faith in Jesus Christ in no uncertain terms. It was a word of truth, their acceptance and appreciation of it as a foundation block upon which to build their lives, that became their basis for accomplishment and success. They held to their convictions based on truth, and the truth sustained them.

"Champions are not men who never fail, but men who never quit," was the word that sustained Ken in his most difficult time of life.

"Change is not change until it is change," is what Rod said pierced his heart and mind.

Sal was struck with the fact that he didn't need to pray for opportunities, but pray to be ready when opportunities came.

For Bee it was, "Perseverance will always outlast persecution," that made a difference in his life.

Words are a medium of manifestation, a means of communication, and a method of revelation. The proverb says, *Timely advice is as lovely as golden apples in a silver basket* (Proverbs 25:11 TLB). The good "word" can mean a singular word, phrase, principle, or a truth from God's Word.

Many times I have made the statement, "Life is composed of our choices and constructed by our words." To change your life, change your choices and the use of your words.

You cannot correct what's wrong in your life by continuing to do the same things that caused the problems. You have to be willing to change. You have to have courage to change. Change is the only constant in maturity. When the men I'm writing about in this book heard truth, a word from God, they used it to make a change in their lives.

They also showed great courage in the face of adversity, uncertainty, or opportunity. They had the courage to admit they needed help. "I don't want to be known as a survivor, but as an overcomer," one declared. There is more to life than just existing. Survivors exist. Overcomers live. But it takes courage to go beyond survival and into life.

Courage is exemplified by walking away from something when you prefer to fight. Courage is also shown by the willingness to fight when you prefer to run. It is wisdom to know the difference. *A man's courage can sustain his broken body, but when courage dies, what hope is left?* (Proverbs 18:14 TLB). In such a manner the proverb describes the essential need for courage.

Courage can come in many shapes and sizes, known in a variety of ways, but it is a necessity in a life of real manhood.

These men also have enough courage to face the reality of their own failures, shortcomings, mistakes, and sins. They are not without flaws, for we are all at best flawed human beings. But their defects, whatever they might be, are not a cause for defeat. They have learned not to major in personal weaknesses, faults, or imperfections, nor let them hinder progress or growth — but to major in their strengths.

They have learned that repentance is not something done once in order to gain faith in God or a passport to heaven, but a lifestyle of putting away the past, to live in the present, and for future benefit.

A courageous man's confidence is not altogether in himself, but in the God Who put him together. Belief, for him, is something to be acted upon. In so doing, it becomes faith. He is not simply an optimist, believing in the power of positive thinking, but a man of substance. Optimism is an attitude. Faith is a substance.

Walking in faith when there is no sign or external evidence that what he is doing is right brings a courageous man through in his most trying moments. That is when his faith is proven to be as pure as gold. A fiery furnace can destroy or purify any matter or quality of life.

When Dino was the only one in the medical profession who believed his daughter was worth saving, he was to have the pleasure of knowing he was right and they were wrong. Standing against the onslaught of unbelief requires a man strong in faith. Peer pressure at any age is always the same. Capitulation's consequences are always the same — allowing someone else to create your world for you.

The emphatic line I wrote in the book *Maximized Manhood* was, "Don't let someone else create your world, for when they do they will always create it too small."[2] Men of courageous manhood are not those who create their own world, or let another do it, but submit to the Creator Who makes all things good.

To face fear, failure, and the future requires a brave heart. Faintheartedness, fearfulness, and fragility of spirit in a man is the bane of every woman and a trial to a wife. God wants men to be consistent, decisive, and strong. Women want the same. Strength is a virtue; weakness a vice.

The realm of decisiveness, more often than not, is where courageous manliness is found. These men are willing to make the tough decisions. Knowledge is translated into power, decision into energy, and courage is translated into virtue. Courage honors; cowardice dishonors.

Sacred writ says, *A double minded man is unstable in all his ways* (James 1:8). That's what struck Robert and helped him out of a life of drugs. The double-minded man is like froth on a wave tossed to and fro, without foundation, never able to provide a quality with which to build a life, family, business, or ministry.

When Suliasi's young men determined to reach every home for Christ in the Solomon Islands, even when it meant entering the region of a primitive cannibalistic tribe from which visitors were never known to return, it took courage added to their faith to make it happen. The results are a series of miracles that almost defy description.

Be strong and of a good courage (Joshua 1:9) is not a brotherly salutation, but a divine exhortation.

In a country where being a man of faith in Christ is tantamount to a governmental death sentence, life is not easy. Yet it is being done in an ordinary way by men who see nothing extraordinary in it. If faith without works is dead, then courage is essential to the life of faith. Heroes of faith never think of themselves as such, but merely see themselves as being obedient to a life of faith. A life of obedient faith is the only life for a real man.

Profiling these men exhaustively would fill a library, so their lives are only highlighted in this book. Not all can be told here — only eternity will allow for such a recounting. Most have never made the headlines in a daily newspaper, been featured on the nightly television news, nor had their picture plastered on a post office wall. They are your friends, neighbors, and your brothers in faith. Each in turn desires to share his experiences with others. I'm doing it with them and for them as I write to you.

The principles of courageous manhood are for every man. They are requisite in manliness. They are yours to learn and to live by.

This book is written in the hope it will encourage you to face your own fears and overcome them; to face the truth and let it change your life; and to maintain integrity in a world of compromise. I hope that some word of truth will bring you the freedom to become greater than ever before, even as it lifted these men to new levels of faith and practice.

❧

P R I N C I P L E S *for* COURAGEOUS MANHOOD

♦ HEROES ARE MEN WHO ACT IN A MOMENT OF TIME ON A NEED GREATER THAN THEMSELVES.

♦ IT TAKES COURAGE TO HOLD CONVICTIONS, TO CHANGE, TO ADMIT NEED, TO FACE REALITY, AND TO MAKE DECISIONS.

♦ CHAMPIONS ARE NOT MEN WHO NEVER FAIL, BUT MEN WHO NEVER QUIT.

♦ CHANGE IS NOT CHANGE UNTIL IT IS CHANGE.

♦ MEN NEED NOT PRAY FOR OPPORTUNITIES, BUT PRAY TO BE READY WHEN OPPORTUNITIES COME.

♦ PERSEVERANCE WILL ALWAYS OUTLAST PERSECUTION.

♦ LIFE IS COMPOSED OF OUR CHOICES AND CONSTRUCTED BY OUR WORDS.

♦ TO CHANGE YOUR LIFE, CHANGE YOUR CHOICES AND THE USE OF YOUR WORDS.

♦ CHANGE IS THE ONLY CONSTANT IN MATURITY.

♦ COURAGE IS EXEMPLIFIED BY WALKING AWAY FROM SOMETHING WHEN YOU WOULD PREFER TO FIGHT. AND COURAGE IS SHOWN BY THE WILLINGNESS TO FIGHT WHEN YOU WOULD PREFER TO RUN.

♦ REPENTANCE IS A LIFESTYLE OF PUTTING AWAY THE PAST, TO LIVE IN THE PRESENT, FOR FUTURE BENEFIT.

♦ OPTIMISM IS AN ATTITUDE; FAITH IS A SUBSTANCE.

♦ DON'T LET SOMEONE ELSE CREATE YOUR WORLD, FOR WHEN THEY DO THEY WILL ALWAYS CREATE IT TOO SMALL.

♦ KNOWLEDGE IS TRANSLATED INTO POWER. DECISION IS TRANSLATED INTO ENERGY. COURAGE IS TRANSLATED INTO VIRTUE.

ONE

KEN MADDEN

COURAGE TO REBUILD

Champions are not those who never fail,
but those who never quit.

Ken wasn't even thinking about losing it all. Losing his friend was too much to bear as it was. He shifted the living weight in his arms and lunged forward, keeping his head down to protect against the snow from the Himalayan storm. Just weeks earlier, mountain climbing in Nepal had seemed a great adventure, something to add with pride to his many summits. But now he only felt fear as he struggled to help carry his buddy down the glacier, under the shadow of Mount Everest.

He thought of Edwin, laughing as they summitted other peaks. He remembered the photo he had at home — a picture of himself with a huge smile lighting his angular face, and standing next to him was an exceptionally well-conditioned 28-year-old Edwin, the epitome of the rugged mountaineer, but wearing a pair of ridiculous black horned-rimmed glasses with no glass in them. That was Edwin. Through his mind ran images of other climbing adventures when he and Edwin successfully summitted peaks in North and South America. They never failed to summit. They were winners!

Ken remembered getting off the plane in Kathmandu. They had so much gear that their team had to rent an entire second bus when they took off from the city through the canyons and drainages to the tiny villages at the base of the enormous, craggy peaks. He remembered a restless Edwin making the villagers laugh in the remote village homes where they stayed before starting the climb. From there they hired lowland porters to carry the gear to the higher altitude — to the Sherpa villages, where porters would help them carry their gear the rest of the way.

Ken figured it must have been only ten days earlier that the climbing team gave the Sherpas the customary sunglasses, Chinese tennis shoes, and wool socks. He and Edwin had laughed at the strange custom because the Sherpas never used their mandatory "gifts." Instead of protecting themselves against the glaring sun or the icy crags that gashed and split their feet, the Sherpas — both men and women — headed off barefoot and bare-eyed over the rugged terrain and through the bitter weather.

Edwin was one of the fittest in the group as they arrived at the high altitude base camp at 17,000 feet. By then their gear was lighter. Almost half of what they originally brought had either been consumed or given away and only the high altitude Sherpas would stay with them for the rest of the climb.

It was upon leaving the advanced high altitude camp that their climb had suddenly ended. Edwin came down with "high altitude pulmonary edema," a sometimes fatal illness every mountaineer risks. He rallied for a day, then worsened. That's when it was determined that Edwin's only hope was to get down to a lower altitude.

Now, base camp seemed a distant hope for the medical help Edwin desperately needed. Ken climbed down the very mountain he'd just scaled days earlier, knowing he could make it — that he had to make it for his friend. Finally, overwhelmed by memories and tired from the steep descent, he helped adjust Edwin onto one of the Sherpas' backs, with another climber balancing the load.

When Edwin seemed to stabilize at the lower base camp, Ken started back up the mountain until his radio crackled. He heard the news that didn't require translation. Edwin was dead. There on the side of the massive Himalayan glacier, the climbing team hacked a grave with pickaxes and buried their climbing friend.

"Hélène, I can't believe I lost him. I did all I could," Ken told his wife two days later when he reached her at advanced base camp.

"We didn't summit. He's dead. Worse, he never accepted Christ. I told him and prayed for him. But I never talked to him strong enough for him to hear me. It's my fault."

Ken's first and only relief came when their plane landed in Colorado. He and Hélène drove to their small ranch outside of town and he fell into a deep sleep, comforted by the familiar surroundings. Years earlier Ken had settled in a Colorado mountain city after a salvation experience in California — the quintessential "Jesus Freak," living in the mountains in a teepee to "forsake all" and follow Christ. In the "forsake all" lifestyle he worked as a carpenter, never allowing himself to follow his ambitions because he believed that to be holy, you had to be poor. It took a painful divorce to awaken him to a fuller picture of the Christ-like life. After the divorce, he developed his own business and started earning a good income as a custom home builder for himself and his new bride, a beautiful, free-spirited outdoorswoman named Hélène.

That was the business he longed to get back to after two months in Nepal. Coming in on a Friday night, Ken decided to work on Saturday.

"I'm sorry about Edwin," his assistant said when Ken showed up at the office.

"Yeah," Ken said, his head hanging. "So what's happening here?"

She handed him a bank ledger and the last month's financial reports. Ken knew he'd left several good projects for his men to complete and had enough new contracts pending to ensure the business would survive his absence. But the bank account showed something different. Ken picked up the financial reports. The tens of thousands in the bank were gone to pay the current debts, no new money had come in, and there were debts he wouldn't be able to pay. With no money available to hold him over until he could get contracts signed and new homes started, the business was no longer viable. He was broke.

Too grief-stricken to react to this newest loss, under too much self-condemnation to stay, Ken returned home to tell Hélène and promise himself, as much as her, that he'd work to get new contracts.

Hélène saw the depression coming. Ken didn't sleep much that weekend, or for months to come. Monday he was out on the job sites, following up leads. Within a short time, he landed two good contracts and slugged away to keep the business afloat. For eighteen months he struggled not only in his business, but also emotionally and spiritually. Often he would wake Hélène in the middle of the night to go outside and walk the snowy paths around their ranch. Fighting depression and thoughts of suicide, looking up at the night shadows of the mountains, they prayed and asked God for help.

Ken finally acknowledged that he couldn't make it. He'd done all he could. He had failed in business. He felt he had failed Edwin. He had failed God. He had failed as an athlete to summit in Nepal. He had failed in one marriage and was now bringing his new wife down with him into his depression. *How many other ways can a man fail?* he wondered. As he prayed, he got a slight feeling, a little nudge, that they should move to Arizona, far from all friends and family, and start over.

Not strong enough to reason or to argue, he followed his feeling. From the mountains he loved, he and Hélène sold everything and moved to the flat desert floor of Arizona. It was the last place on earth he wanted to be. When he arrived, a man he met at the church they attended had also just suffered a business failure. Together, they went to a men's event in Phoenix. There Ken heard something that stuck in his mind: "Champions are not those who never fail, but those who never quit."

Ken wrote the words on index cards and taped them to his bathroom mirror, his dashboard, and his night stand. He kept those words in front of him hourly, prayed regularly with Hélène, and started over as a humble carpenter. Starting from scratch, Ken eventually launched a custom home business once again. He studied out the terrain and built quality homes, using the desert as a backdrop, and completing the homes with desert landscapes and motifs.

He was satisfied with the results, but within months, the real estate market collapsed and he couldn't make a profit. All he could do was not quit. "You won't fail if you don't quit," he told himself daily, hourly.

He left home every morning and fought his way through every day. Climbing the mountain to emotional and financial recovery proved more difficult than the Himalayas. Money was scarce, tension high, and the twin weights of failure and sorrow exhausting. One night, Ken walked into his backyard and looked up at the sky.

"God," he said, "everything that could go wrong has gone wrong. I know one thing is true — that You have never left me nor forsaken me. Even if You forsake me, I will never leave You."

Putting God first above all else, helped Ken see his life from God's perspective. He realized his life was God's problem, not just his own, and if anything good was to happen, it would be God's doing.

One day his secretary stopped him as he came in off the job, sweaty and dirty.

"I've been looking at this magazine," she said, holding up a home builders' magazine. "There's a contest here that I think you should enter."

"Okay," he said wearily as he went to his desk and sat down. A few minutes later, she was at the door to his office.

"There's some more besides that one," she said.

"How much do they cost to enter?"

"Well, if you do them all, it will wipe out the bank account."

"We don't have enough to buy anything else," he said. "Go ahead and enter them."

Within three months Ken's company won all five national awards and suddenly his phones lit up. As Ken and Hélène drove to receive one of Ken's awards in front of a crowded hotel ballroom, they laughed ironically at their situation.

"I'm being named one of the top builders in the nation," he said, "and I might not be in business next week!"

As they drove, they prayed for God to give Ken courage to do what he needed to do that night. When he heard his introduction, he walked to the microphone.

"I have to say first that Jesus Christ is the reason I've received this award...."

Later he would say that acknowledging Jesus in front of his peers was a greater joy than any mountain summit. Today, the time and energy once consumed by depression, grief, and anxiety is used for reaching out to other men to see them saved, well-taught, and successful. And his home building business is now immensely successful, winning many awards, including the most prestigious in the industry, the "Home of the Year." Ken doesn't climb physical mountains anymore. He gets his kicks instead from his family, his work, and his ministry to other men.

I first met Ken at a meeting in Newport Beach, California. He stood to introduce himself and his wife with a few brief words and sat down. I learned over the years that this was not all there was to this unique man, nor was he a man of few words. Today he is regarded as one of the foremost custom home builders in the United States, and he has won well over twenty awards as "number one" in the nation.

Truth changed Ken's life. He heard it. He read it. But more than that, he clung to it like a rope. Suspended over a chasm of failure and total collapse, day by day the truth sustained him. Just one sentence with the weight of eternal truth began to rebuild his life:

"Champions are not those who never fail, but those who never quit."

One truth can change a man's life when he adheres to it in faith and practice. Too many men hear truth but don't make it part of their lives. The love of the truth is the criterion for spiritual life. Truth is the foundation for the way you live and the life you have. Any lie has inherent terminality, but truth will never die.

Trust is extended to the limit of truth and no more. To trust in what is not true is to trust in a lie. And no lie can serve the purposes of God in your life.

Ken's respect for truth made him become a man of his word. People could depend on what he said. So those he did business with referred others to him. It took visceral fortitude, otherwise known as "guts," to tell the truth when others were getting the clients by promising what they could not deliver. What they could not deliver, Ken could. Today he has the business others want and cannot get. He was trustworthy, so he was constantly given more trust. The reward of the trustworthy is more trust.

Jesus talked about the difference between building a house on a rock or on sand. It's always the foundation that upholds the building, never the superstructure. A love for truth will build a rock-solid foundation for success in business, marriage, friendship, fathering, and ministry. The rock upon which true life is built is the Lord Jesus Christ.

Our reverence for God's Word makes us reverent of our word. Ken has learned that his word is his bond, so men listen to him when he speaks. When we revere our word, others listen when we talk about reverence for God's Word.

Ken is a man's man. But he had to overcome failure. By so doing, he found another truth, that the greatest antidote to failure is success.

After Ken started winning awards and his business began to thrive, he embraced yet another true principle and adopted it into his life. Scripture says: *Thine own friend, and thy father's friend, forsake not; neither go into thy brother's house in the day of thy calamity: for better is a neighbour that is near than a brother far off* (Proverbs 27:10).

The principle is, "Funds come from friends."

When Ken heard it, he practiced it. He stopped looking for customers, clients, or buyers, and began to make friends of those with whom he did business. As he made friends and sought to give them what they wanted rather than telling them what they needed, as he offered godly counsel rather than good advice, they introduced him to their friends as a friend. His friends multiplied. Building on that truth took his business to a new level.

Truth also had to overcome a lie from Ken's early Christian life. Ken once believed that poverty and holiness were synonymous and that he was not worthy to be prosperous. Today he realizes that God sends contracts his way because God can trust him to use the income they produce for His kingdom. As I write, Ken has dozens of homes in construction, averaging over one million dollars per home. Instead of fighting feelings of being "unworthy" of such prosperity, Ken now realizes that his income is for God's purposes, not his own. He's not afraid to earn it anymore, seeing it as potential for doing good in God's kingdom. *Therefore to him that knoweth to do good, and doeth it not, to him it is sin* (James 4:17).

Learning how to receive from God changed my own life. Years ago, through a disastrous attempt at helping another ministry, I invested everything I had and lost it all. Returning from the East Coast of the U.S. to the West, my wife and I had nothing but our Bibles, a car, and a few personal possessions.

When we arrived in California, God sovereignly instituted a forty-day fast in my life. Between the twenty-first and thirty-eighth days, God taught me what has been a foundational truth for my life and His ministry now called the Christian Men's Network.

Nancy and I were living in a small, two-bedroom home when our two daughters came back home to live and her father came to visit. Too many people in such a small place! I prayed about another house, and Nancy searched the newspaper. We found one just up the hill from us, a lovely three bedroom home on a corner in a secluded community. Though we prayed over it and felt good about it, I thought it was too much money for us.

As I walked the beach, prayed, and read my Bible, the words leaped out at me, that if you know to do good and don't do it — it is sin. I read it again and it seemed to say, "To him that knoweth to prosper and doeth it not, to him it is sin." To prosper was to do good.

Then I heard the Lord speak to my heart, "If I asked you to move into a one bedroom home from your two bedroom, would you do it?"

I answered, "Yes, Lord!"

"Then why won't you move into a three bedroom if I ask you to?" Immediately I saw the issue wasn't in bedrooms or houses, but rather it was, would I obey God? Then another passage came to mind.

Blessed is the man that walketh not in the counsel of the ungodly, nor standeth in the way of sinners, nor sitteth in the seat of the scornful. But his delight is in the law of the LORD; and in his law doth he meditate day and night. And he shall be like a tree planted by the rivers of water, that bringeth forth his fruit in his season; his leaf also shall not wither; and whatsoever he doeth shall prosper (Psalm 1:1-3).

Prosperity is the natural, sequentially-ordered result of righteousness in life. It is not a ten-letter obscenity as some would expound, but the result of living God's way. Refusal to allow God to prosper us individually, corporately, or in ministry is to regress, not progress, and do disservice for God's kingdom. *My true disciples produce bountiful harvests. This brings great glory to my Father* (John 15:8 TLB).

Faith took hold of Ken's heart, and courage enabled him to hold his convictions. Truth set him free and also held him from error. Ken's intrepidity for truth gave him integrity in life, which led to every good thing.

P R I N C I P L E S *for* COURAGEOUS MANHOOD

♦ "CHAMPIONS ARE NOT THOSE WHO NEVER FAIL, BUT THOSE WHO NEVER QUIT."

♦ THE LOVE OF THE TRUTH IS THE CRITERION FOR SPIRITUAL LIFE.

♦ TRUTH IS THE FOUNDATION FOR THE WAY YOU LIVE, AND THE LIFE YOU HAVE.

♦ TRUST IS EXTENDED TO THE LIMIT OF TRUTH AND NO MORE.

♦ TO TRUST IN WHAT IS NOT TRUE IS TO TRUST IN A LIE.

♦ NO LIE CAN SERVE THE PURPOSES OF GOD.

♦ THE REWARD OF THE TRUSTWORTHY IS MORE TRUST.

♦ OUR REVERENCE FOR GOD'S WORD MAKES US REVERENT OF OUR WORD.

♦ THE GREATEST ANTIDOTE TO FAILURE IS SUCCESS.

♦ FUNDS COME FROM FRIENDS.

♦ PROSPERITY IS THE NATURAL, SEQUENTIALLY ORDERED RESULT OF RIGHTEOUSNESS IN LIFE.

TWO

DINO J. DELAPORTAS, M.D.

COURAGE TO
CHOOSE

The only true freedom we have in life is the freedom to choose.
But once we choose, we become the servants of our choice.

"They think there's a problem," Kathy told Dino over the phone. She had just completed an ultrasound test to check the due date of their second child. As a physician, Dino knew what a miracle it was for Kathy to be pregnant again. They had only one child alive after six pregnancies. His friends all thought they were crazy to keep trying.

"Go ahead and adopt! Or get in vitro done," they told Dino. But Dino found strength in the story of Jairus from the New Testament. (See Mark 5:22-42.) Everyone was getting healed all around Jairus, while his daughter lay at home slowly dying. Jairus had to fight jealousy and impatience to see God work in his family. When he finally approached Jesus, Jesus looked at him and said, "Fear not, only believe." If Jairus hadn't waited, if he'd been impatient, he would have missed the miracle in his daughter's life.

Dino took the lesson of the story to heart and he and Kathy decided to wait patiently on God for His miracles in their lives. After a fourth tubal pregnancy, they conceived what they believed would be their son David's little sister. One ultrasound test confirmed their suspicions — they were going to have a girl. Now Kathy was at Johns Hopkins Hospital to get a more precise test run, just to verify a due date so she and Dino could plan. Dino couldn't imagine what "problem" Kathy could possibly be referring to. Because he understood medicine, his first inclination was to think it was something minor — something he would be able to help fix.

"I'll give you to the doctor," Kathy said.

Dr. Snyder took the phone. Dino knew who she was. She wrote the book on fetal echocardiology.

"Dr. Delaportas," she said gravely, "it looks like an A-V Canal Defect."

In an instant, Dino's medical education flashed through his mind and he remembered the disease. It was also called endocardial cushion defect and had only a 20 percent chance of recovery.

"And, there's an 80 percent chance she's Down's Syndrome as well," the doctor said.

A fire lit up in Dino. *No, this isn't going to happen to my child!* he shrieked inside. He hung up the phone and walked into his clinic manager's office to tell her. As he said the words, he heard the Holy Spirit say to his heart, "You're going to walk through the fiery furnace, but I'm going to be with you."

He left the office early to meet Kathy at home. When he walked into the house, she was crying.

"I'll be okay," she said. "I just need to grieve and get it out of my system."

Kathy's doctors and Dino's colleagues suggested an amniocentesis test that would determine the extent of the damage and give them the option of aborting the child. But Dino and

Kathy stood firm against the pressure — they were going to have this child no matter what. They didn't need further tests.

Katie was born at 12:30 A.M. on August 31, 1994. She was examined thoroughly by the team of medical experts awaiting her delivery.

"She has the heart defect they previously described," a stern-faced doctor told Dino at 3:30 A.M. "And she has Down's Syndrome."

Looking down at the tiny body in front of him, the first thought that came to Dino's mind was, "She's better off dead." And the second was, "God never answered your prayers."

At that point, Dino had to make his first choice. He could choose to believe a lie — a lie against God and against life — or he could believe with the faith he'd built through years of Bible study and worship. It was his choice, and he knew it. Knowing that it had certainly been months since he felt any prayer had been answered, he couldn't help but agree, but he knew that agreeing with death would cost Katie her destiny. He was inwardly pulled, feeling the struggle over Katie's life being fought on the battleground of his mind.

Pacing the walkway outside, Dino cried out, "Why God? Why is this happening to her?" Instantly, he felt the same Holy Spirit Who told him about the fiery furnace well up within him and speak gently to his heart again, "This is only a snapshot of her life; it's not her whole life."

Dino remembered a principle he had learned: The only true freedom we have in life is the freedom to choose, but once we choose, we become the servants of our choice. He returned to Kathy's bedside and said, "It's going to be fine,

Kathy." They cried and prayed together, determining to make a life for Katie, no matter what the cost.

Three days later a social worker came to do a case study, a routine task for severe birth defects. After talking with them and filling out forms she gave her opinion.

"You're going to have to get over your denial," she said firmly.

"What denial?" Dino asked incredulously. "I'm an internist. I'm not in denial. I know better than you what's going on with my little girl."

The woman continued to look at him, expressionless.

Dino marched her down the hall to the windows outside the neonatal intensive care unit. Pointing to his baby, filled with tubes and surrounded by monitors, he said, "Look at her! She's beautiful! I would adopt her!"

The woman blinked, then looked at Dino and said, "Most people aren't nearly this far along at this point." Then she shut her folder and left.

Five difficult months later they were able to take Katie to Johns Hopkins for the reconstructive heart surgery she needed. Kathy had nursed her at home, wheeling around the pole with the nasogastric feeding tube on it in one hand, while she balanced her little baby in the other, and kept up with their toddler, David. Katie had needed three hospitalizations during her first five months because she couldn't breathe and swallow at the same time. And since Katie couldn't eat, Kathy's daily routine with her was grueling.

Between Katie's hospitalizations, Dino had scheduled to take the Boards to receive his credentials in the sub-specialty of Infectious Disease. Most doctors took them right after training, and even then there was a 40 percent failure rate. Dino had been too busy for fourteen years, but when the Lord convicted him not to wait any longer, he finally hit the books and decided to tackle the exams. Then came Katie. Dino could have canceled and received his money back, but he believed that God knew what the timing would be months earlier when Dino scheduled them. He decided to study, take them, and trust that God would see him through.

All through Katie's hospitalizations, Dino sat in waiting areas with his books open, grabbing precious moments whenever he could to study the highly specialized field. The pressure was tremendous, but when the time came, he endured the eight-hour exam. After it was over, every colleague seemed to be watching him — the Christian who took the Boards fourteen years late. No one expected him to pass. Even doctors he didn't know well, when he passed them in hospital corridors, would greet him with, "Have you heard about your Boards yet?"

Dino and Kathy continued to pray over Katie's heart, trusting that when it came time for the surgery, they'd find it was healed. Instead, the doctors spent over seven hours in surgery with their precious Katie.

"The good news is that the surgery went well," the head surgeon told Dino when they finally came out of surgery. "But her heart was in much worse shape than we thought. If she makes it through the night, she may have a chance."

Dino explained to Kathy in laymen's terms that the baby had only one heart chamber out of four. The surgeons had built four heart chambers and two valves, and while they thought the repair went well, they didn't think she could survive such extensive work.

"Kathy, go back to your mother's and try to get some sleep," Dino told her. "I'll stay here, and I'll call you if something happens."

Dino paced the floor in the waiting room. He prayed constantly, feeling the struggle of choosing between believing God for a miracle or falling into the quagmire of hopelessness that seemed so inviting. Finally he walked into the pediatric intensive care unit to see if he could find out anything. Eight doctors stood in a knot together, grim-faced, working out what could be done to save her. They motioned for Dino to sit down. As he sat, he heard their report from the echocardiogram. The medicines they were giving her weren't working. They couldn't get the heart to respond. Dino felt like his insides were being kicked with each new report he heard. Over an hour passed before they addressed him directly.

"Her heart is not pumping," Dr. Cameron told Dino. "She's at the edge of a cliff. One little thing goes wrong, and we lose her."

One of Kathy's babies had died due to SIDS. All the others but David died in ectopic pregnancies that required surgery. So many hospitals. So much death. Dino didn't know how his wife could handle losing another child. Regardless of how hard he fought, hopelessness, despair, and doom enveloped him.

"God," he said crying, "I can't call Kathy and tell her Katie's dying."

He went to the waiting area called Kathy at her mother's house. "Honey," he said softly. "You're not going to sleep anyway, so why don't you come on back to the hospital."

He didn't tell her how bad it looked. He wanted to choose to believe, not to give way to his fears by saying anything negative. He hung up the phone and wandered into the room where his little Katie lay — hooked up to multiple machines, with eight tubes in her tiny body, looking like something out of NASA. He realized this was it. Either God did something now or it was over. He hadn't seen an answer to prayer in months. Now, his daughter was dying. He thought of Jairus' patience again, and Jesus' words to Jairus came clearly to his mind, "Fear not, only believe, and she will be made whole."

He focused on the Lord, trying wholly to believe that Katie would live. He got no answer, no promise of any kind. But something within him started to change. Without emotion or any external evidence, he realized he was having an encounter with God.

Reaching through the tangle of wires and tubes, his hand found Katie's tiny foot. It was cold. He quickly scanned the monitors to see if there was any sign of life. There was. As he looked at her, feeling that cold little foot, he remembered the choices he'd made so far. And now again, he had a choice to make. He thought of the verse from Deuteronomy, which said, "I set before you life and death; therefore choose life." (See Deuteronomy 30:19.)

"Katie," he said out loud. "I choose life, Katie. You're not going to die. You're going to live."

He was standing in front of the mass of tubes, believing with all his heart for Katie's healing, when Kathy slipped up beside him. She saw her little girl dying and started sobbing. Dino held her tightly.

"Don't say anything," he said. "Just let yourself cry."

Dr. Cameron met them as they went back to the waiting room. He pulled Dino aside.

"I'm going to hang one more drug," he said. "I know it won't work, but it may buy us some time."

Dino didn't know what was going to happen, but he knew the cloud of despair had left him. Dino and Kathy waited, praying in the waiting room. Twenty minutes later the doctor walked back in.

"I think we have a response," he said.

As they walked back into Katie's room, that cold little foot was now pink. Dino touched it. Katie was warm. They were on their way to their miracle! Dr. Cameron was incredulous, choosing to stay another hour into the night to see if the miracle could really be sustained. Dino walked him to the elevator when he finally left.

"I have no medical explanation for what happened tonight," Dr. Cameron said. *None,* thought Dino, *except that Jesus did for us what He did for Jairus when we chose to believe.*

When Katie stabilized a week later, Dino headed for home to return to work at his clinic. He was on the phone to Kathy, who was telling him how much Katie was improving, when he shuffled through the mail and saw the envelope from the Boards. Dino thought, "No, God, I can't take any more right now." He opened it with Kathy on the other end of the phone giving moral support. A silence followed the opening of the letter. Then —

"I knocked them dead, Kathy," he said with joy and relief. "I passed easily."

For almost three years, Katie's life has been a long, arduous battle for Dino's family, but that's still just what they are — a family. Theirs is a story of courage and faith that has touched whole hospitals, and an entire medical community is still astounded at Dino's resolve.

Kathy believes her little girl will one day excel, not just become average. Katie was able to learn sign language because, although she's in speech therapy, it is still difficult for her to speak. Katie's diagnosis has been upgraded from being severely retarded to having only mild to moderate retardation. Her last hospitalization came almost a year ago. Her eating program is strenuous, even capturing headlines in their local newspaper, but Kathy is championing Katie's cause.

When Dino shows people Katie's snapshots in his wallet, he always remembers that's all her life has been so far — a series of snapshots, not the whole film. His medical friends realize more than others the choices Dino had, and they respect him for choosing life.

Just a few months ago, Dino, Kathy, David, and Katie were presented to a group of medical students as a case history. On one hand, the lesson was about a family coping with severe birth defects. On the other, Dino realizes their lives are a testimony, teaching others that life is worthwhile, and a family can survive.

Dino is living on a level he had never known before Katie entered his life. He has grown to that level since I've known him and become an example of courageous manhood to others all around him.

All of life is lived on levels and arrived at in stages — whether in education, marriage, business or our Christian life. It was so in the life of Israel when they left Egypt to journey to Canaan. *These are the stages of the journeys of the Israelites.... Moses recorded their starting places...stage by stage* (Numbers 33:1,2 AMP).

Dino learned a principle, but only when he put it into practice did he rise to a new level. He was rising to new levels in his medical practice, and God was taking him to new levels in his Christian walk as well. He learned to walk by faith and not by sight.

Light shines brightest in the darkest hour of night. The most beautiful flowers are birthed in the dirt and darkness of earth's soil. A human life is formed in darkness and water to be birthed to live in air and light. Dino's darkest hour became the greatest time of his life. He proved God, and God proved him.

Conversion takes place in both the natural and the supernatural. In each, God is the Creator. Conversion is both instant and constant. We are converted to Christ for salvation, then continually converted in our minds to the revelation of His Word. Dino was converted in his believing by taking God at His Word, and is continually converted as he sees a progressive miracle unfold.

As he paced the corridors of the hospital in his darkest hour, he was walking in the light of God's Word. "Fear not," was God's salutation to the virgin Mary when Christ's birth was announced, which was the same salutation God gave to Dino. "Choose life" was the command he had to follow. Those words were the substance of faith — a bright beam like a ray of truth from heaven to his soul. That was all he needed. It was a new stage in his manhood. In the moment he stood in front of Katie's bed and won the struggle to believe in God, he rose to a new level of faith.

In their trial, Dino and Kathy never complained or murmured against God. They knew murmuring was one of the five sins that kept Israel out of Canaan, one that would keep them from their Promised Land as well. They knew God loved their daughter even more than they did.

Crisis is normal to life. Dino prepared for his crisis by diligent study of God's Word, being faithful in daily prayer, and staying in unity with his wife. He understood that agreement is the power of life. His agreement with God and His Word and his agreement with his wife in their daily walk with God prepared him for his greatest test.

Preparation is like health insurance. You can never get health insurance after the illness hits, and in the same way, you cannot prepare after the crisis occurs. All you can do is be ready when it comes. Failure to prepare is preparation for failure.

Dino had learned that the only true freedom we have in life is the freedom to choose. But once we choose, we become the servants of our choice. It was the choice he made in patient faith that determined his daughter's destiny. A choice that was made spontaneously and rightly because it was rooted and grounded in the character that had been established — not from medical school, but in the school of the Spirit, schooling that is done by God's Spirit as the Word is implanted in mind and heart. The tablets on which God's commandments were written were the tablets of Dino's heart.

Life is composed of our choices and constructed by our words. Never was that more true than in Dino's darkest hour when he made the right choice and said the right words.

"You are an inspiration," people tell him.

"I don't understand that," is Dino's reply. "All I try to do is just make it through one more day. I pray, 'God give me faith and courage for one more day,' and He does it — day after day."

Of such days a life is made.

One day at a time.

One level at a time.

One choice at a time.

As you read this, the circumstances of your life may be just what God needs to take you to the next level. Instead of rejecting the situation and murmuring against God, why not accept it and believe God to turn it into a blessing?

Prove your manhood. Show yourself a man — a courageous man!

◆❖◆

PRINCIPLES *for* COURAGEOUS MANHOOD

◆ ALL OF LIFE IS LIVED ON LEVELS AND ARRIVED AT IN STAGES.

◆ CRISIS IS NORMAL TO LIFE.

◆ AGREEMENT IS THE POWER OF LIFE.

◆ FAILURE TO PREPARE IS PREPARATION FOR FAILURE.

- LIFE IS COMPOSED OF OUR CHOICES AND CONSTRUCTED BY OUR WORDS.

- THE ONLY TRUE FREEDOM WE HAVE IN LIFE IS THE FREEDOM TO CHOOSE, BUT ONCE WE CHOOSE, WE BECOME THE SERVANTS OF OUR CHOICE.

THREE

KEVIN DYSON

COURAGE TO
HONOR

*You will always reap what you sow, but you
won't always reap in the same way you sowed.*

Kevin and Joy were elated. All they needed were cursory physical exams to prove to the United States government that they did not have any contagious diseases, and their emigration would be final. They would miss their children and grandchildren, but they'd see them often as they returned to New Zealand and Southeast Asia to teach at the many Bible colleges they had helped establish. It was this work that took them abroad to the U.S. The international network of schools they had founded was the culmination of their life's work, but the organization had now grown too large to be headquartered in their New Zealand homeland easily. When their friends recommended relocating to the States, God had confirmed it to their hearts.

Parting was sad, but the futures of thousands of students in dozens of nations hinged on Kevin and Joy's willingness to move. For Kevin it was a natural act. He'd denied his own desires and made many major changes in pursuit of God's will throughout his life.

After leaving home at an early age, he had been led to Christ while still a young man. With an innate desire to pursue excellence and follow a calling to preach, Kevin began his theological studies at a Methodist college and finally graduated to become a pastor in a different denomination. From teaching and pastoring, he launched the Bible training program that became, in 1978, New Covenant International Bible College.

A dozen years later, he resigned all his other posts to concentrate full time on the international college. That's when it became apparent that they would have to relocate to the U.S. to continue the work. Heartsick about leaving her family, Joy nonetheless made the tough decision with Kevin, and together they set their course for the U.S.

Kevin and Joy went to an old pre-World War II building in Auckland to have their physicals. It was the clinic the U.S. government directed them to. They surmised from its decaying state that the U.S. government contract must be the only thing keeping it in existence.

After their initial tests, they were called back to talk with a doctor. They walked down the wide passage with its high ceilings, brass doorknobs, and oak panels to meet a doctor wearing a short white coat with a stethoscope in his top pocket. He quickly ushered them into his room, as if he'd been waiting for them. Sitting down to talk, Kevin could sense the man was ill at ease.

"I have the report here from your medical application," the doctor said with a thick Scottish brogue. "The U.S. government wants to make sure you are aware of the medical condition you have, Mr. Dyson."

"The what?" Kevin asked. He squeezed Joy's hand to reassure her, a gentle habit developed over thirty years of marriage. Instantly he thought of the heart pains he sometimes had, and a small cloud of worry arose in one part of his mind.

"Have you ever been a heavy smoker?" the Scottish doctor asked.

"Not since I was a teenager," Kevin answered.

"Have you ever had tuberculosis?"

"No."

"Well, we're going to have to send you back for further CAT scans before we can be sure of anything," the doctor said.

"What exactly are you looking for?" Kevin asked.

"We believe you may have asbestosis. Have you ever been around asbestos?"

"Yes," Kevin answered. "As a teenager I used to work at a power station, wrapping asbestos rope around the boiler piping. But that was years ago. I haven't been around asbestos since I left that job as a young man, a boy really."

"It takes about thirty years for it to show up in the lungs," the doctor said softly. No one said anything so he continued. "Look, Mr. Dyson, my best advice to you is to go home, pay up your insurance policy, put your will in order, and take an extended holiday with your grandchildren."

"Why so drastic?" Kevin asked.

"You will need to see a specialist to confirm it, but your lungs are scarred and diseased. You have symptoms similar to emphysema, which will possibly turn into lung cancer. You probably have about three years."

Kevin and Joy walked out of the dusty building into the bright sunlight in complete disbelief. "Well," Kevin said, "we'll just keep on doing what we know to do and trust God with the rest."

CAT scans followed that confirmed the first diagnosis, but Kevin and Joy continued their plans to move. Kevin signed emigration forms promising not to become a dependent of the government when he moved to the U.S. They talked together of believing God for healing and prayed often. All their friends around the world were praying with them. But subconsciously, the little cloud of worry in Kevin's mind was growing into a thunderstorm. He knew instinctively he probably didn't even have three years. As the months passed, his skin grew gray, his chest pains increased, and his breathing became strained. Joy saw the change in her husband and tried to cheer him on, reminding him of the work ahead of them — work that gave so much to live for.

"Pastor Kong Hee is waiting for us to come teach at the school in Singapore," Kevin reminded Joy a few months after the diagnosis. "I think we need to consider it."

"We can't possibly consider it with your condition," Joy insisted. She was desperately concerned that the smallest physical exertion, even breathing, drained her husband and left him too weak to move.

Kevin wanted to pray for healing. He wanted to believe God was bigger than any problem. But the doctor's words ran through his mind every morning when he awoke, and during sleepless nights — *Pay up your insurance. Put your will in order. Go have fun with the grandchildren.* The required respiratory tests revealed his health was growing worse, with only 45 percent use of his lungs.

A special crusade rolled into town that Kevin had wanted to be part of. He had helped organize it in its inception. Still very active in ministry, he went to the meetings and sat with the other Christian leaders on the front row.

"The Bible talks about sowing and reaping," the minister said in his sermon. "You reap what you sow. But the interesting thing is, you don't always reap in the exact same way that you sowed. Let me show you."

Kevin had his pen out to take notes. Being a Bible scholar himself, most good teaching triggered even more thoughts and he'd scribble down notes of things to look up when he got home. As he listened to the minister that day, he wasn't sure exactly where he was going with his message, but he never expected what was coming next.

"Look at the very words of Jesus and I'll show you what I mean. When Jesus said to honor thy father and mother in Luke 18:20, He was quoting Exodus 20:12, which says, *Honour thy father and thy mother: that thy days may be long upon the land which the Lord thy God giveth thee.* There is a promise that it will go well with you and you will have a long life if you honor your parents. You are to give honor first."

A thunderbolt hit Kevin. His mind raced back to his childhood, his dad's violent outbursts that drove him from home at an early age and eventually brought his mother to obtain a legal separation. He remembered that after his conversion, he had made a conscientious effort to honor both his parents, dividing his attentions equally even after they were parted.

His mind came back to the meeting as the minister repeated the verse, then asked the assembly to rehearse it.

"What do you sow?"

The people in the meeting called out in unison, "Honor."

"And what do you reap?"

Kevin whispered as he joined the congregation, "long life." He could hardly hear the rest of the sermon. Memories washed through his mind like fluid streams. He remembered how he'd made things right with his dad and had helped support his mom, how he had continued to honor them to the present day. Internally, he knew he had a promise from God for a long life. The cloud in his mind was vanquished in the pure light of God's Word.

"Joy," he called when he got home that night. "We need to pack. We're going to Singapore!"

Kevin excitedly told her of God's promise. "Joy," he said, "it came so clear to me, so startlingly brilliant, that death and life are in the power of the tongue. (See Proverbs 18:21.) The death in the words of the doctors has just been replaced by the life in the words of God. Let's go!"

They left two weeks later and ministered in the City Harvest Bible Training Centre in Singapore for four straight weeks, four hours per day, with special additional classes in the evenings. Kevin spoke three to four times in churches every Sunday. When they returned to New Zealand, Joy was exhausted but Kevin was invigorated. Radiance replaced the pallor on his face and vigor replaced his slowed gait.

The promise of God's Word was becoming real in Kevin's life. The seed he had planted of honoring his mother and father was giving him a harvest of life. Kevin and Joy moved to the United States and set up the headquarters for the school in Florida. Although at first Kevin was required to return to New Zealand for an annual checkup, the doctors evenutally told him not to come back for a few years because his lungs were within 5 percent of normal.

Ninety thousand students are currently studying in the schools Kevin helped start in fifty-four nations. Kevin and Joy have twelve wonderful grandchildren whom they see often. They have resided in Florida for many years.

❁

Kevin and his wife Joy have lived a life of sowing and reaping. They learned you will always reap what you sow, but you won't always reap in the same manner in which or where you sow. God's moral compensation is done in a divine manner. He always gives back more than you give, because God will be a debtor to no man.

We met when Kevin was still pastoring a local church in New Zealand. He had a desire to disciple men and educate his parishioners, and others, in both secular and sacred fields. His passion is still to see others stand on the Word of God with a right understanding of its truth and doctrine.

Kevin also wants to see Christians properly prepared to work and provide for and raise a family. The Bible is a family book. God is revealed as "God the Father." Believers comprise His family. Kevin hungered to see those in his church family have every advantage possible to be more than average.

Little did he realize when his teaching was taking place with a handful of people in that cold auditorium in Auckland, it would eventually become a worldwide university. "Despise not the day of small beginnings," is the admonishment in Scripture. (See Zechariah 4:10.) He did not despise it then, nor does he now with campuses on almost every continent of the world. It has taken courage added to his faith every step of the way.

Sickly, and subject to the prospects of an early death, he heard and obeyed God's Word. *Honour thy father and thy mother: that thy days may be long upon the land which the Lord thy God giveth thee* (Exodus 20:12).

The word "honor" can be applied many ways, have many meanings, and can be used wisely or foolishly. God never uses any word foolishly, carelessly, or unwisely. His creative power is in His words; therefore, they are used with divine authority and meaning.

Consider some usage and meanings.

"He did the honorable thing." He did what was right and true.

"Your Honor." A title denoting a person's office, position or place in life.

"You have the honor." Means your turn to tee off first when playing golf.

"Do the honors." Talks about being a host when guests arrive.

"In honor of." A meeting to show respect and admiration for someone.

"On my honor." A pledge based on personal and moral integrity.

When God says to "honor" your father and mother, He is talking about a moral obligation to respect your parents. So strong is God's concern for the family and society, He made the relationship between parent and child a commandment. It is a commandment that carries a promise with it. It is called "the first commandment with promise." (See Ephesians 6:2,3.) It is one of the ten commandments which formed the foundation for the moral law given by Moses to Israel. (See Exodus 20:12.) It has the force of God in it.

When the Pharisees perverted the commandment by their tradition, they were excoriated by our Lord's denunciation of them. The Pharisees were encouraging people to make special "Corban" offerings at the expense of the care and consideration of their parents.

When an offering was declared "Corban," something dedicated to use in the Temple, it was a special offering and could not be withdrawn or taken back. By so doing, the Pharisees' tradition took precedence over God's commandment. It was a violation of God's Word, and Jesus denounced them for dishonoring God: *For Moses said, Honour thy father and thy mother...But ye say, If a man shall say to his father or mother, It is Corban, that is to say, a gift, by whatsoever thou mightest be profited by me; he shall be free. And ye suffer him no more to do ought for his father or his mother; making the word of God of none effect through your tradition, which ye have delivered: and many such like things do ye* (Mark 7:10-13).

The promise of a long life was the promise of God Kevin stood on for his healing and the longevity of his life. God's

Word has proven true in that he is almost totally healed, and he is still ministering around the world.

What he sowed so lavishly to the few, he is reaping from the many. What he sowed as a son, he reaps as a man.

P R I N C I P L E S *for* COURAGEOUS MANHOOD

♦ YOU WILL ALWAYS REAP WHAT YOU SOW, BUT YOU WON'T ALWAYS REAP IN THE SAME WAY YOU SOWED.

♦ GOD WILL BE A DEBTOR TO NO MAN.

FOUR

ROD ANDERSON

COURAGE TO
CHANGE

Change is not change until it is change.

"Don't let him know he's going to die," he heard his sisters say in quiet hushes as they tiptoed into his hospital room. He had complications from a heroin overdose and doctors had already pronounced him dead once. Rod jolted in the bed, unable to communicate, but trying to scream at them. One of the tubes attached to his throat popped off in his struggle. The nurse quieted him, and his mother and sisters spoke to him with hopeful words, telling him everything was going to be all right. Their words brought tears to his eyes. His family had always been there whenever he needed them. He loved them, and didn't know why he'd developed a heroin addiction coming from such a loving home.

He had a lot of questions about life, but for now, all he knew was that he had to get out of the hospital. Two young women and a young man who had known Rod in high school heard about his situation and came to the hospital to pray. Twice more he was pronounced dead, but miraculously he recovered. The Russian doctor working on Rod refused to give up. He told Rod's family that Rod had the strongest will to live he'd ever seen.

After eleven days in a coma and another thirty recovering, Rod was finally released to a joyous family that welcomed him home with open arms — and to an angry police force that thought the community of Bakersfield would be better off if this scumbag was dead. The first thing Rod wanted was to shoot up again, but he was determined to stay clean.

The police had busted him twice for "profiteering," and one more bust would violate the "three strikes" law in California, allowing them to put him away for years. They hired an informant named Mingo to befriend Rod's dad. Mingo would play pool with him, and Rod's gentle father felt he was doing the young man a favor by being his friend. But when his dad was out of the room, the man would target Rod.

"Man, I haven't got high in so long. I wish I could get some just once," Mingo would say to Rod. Rod ignored him many times, but finally Mingo's persistence paid off.

"Okay, I know where to get you some," Rod said. He met Mingo at the prearranged liquor store, but as he handed him the bag, he saw in Mingo's eyes he'd been had. Mingo snatched the bag and instantly a camper parked across the street opened and armed officers sprinted toward them. Rod jumped in his car and somehow outran the police, weaving his way into the mountains to a friend's empty cabin.

He immediately called everyone he knew to warn them about the "snitch." Then he thought things through. He knew he'd be arrested and face a minimum of twenty-five years. But he'd never been convicted of a violent crime before, so if he committed a violent crime, the lesser drug charges would be dropped. The prisons were so overcrowded, he knew he'd only do about seven and a half years for murder, which beat the drug rap by far. It all added up.

Rod left the cabin intent on killing Mingo. He went to the Methadone clinic where he knew he could find him.

"Hey, where's Mingo?" he asked one of his acquaintances with fake nonchalance.

"He left about five minutes ago," the man said, looking strangely at Rod. "Hey, you heard about your dad, right?"

"What about my dad?"

"Man, he's dying. He had a stroke and he's in the hospital right now."

Rod ran to a pay phone and called one of his sisters.

"Hello?" she said, her voice strained and wavering, confirming with one word Rod's fear.

"It's Rod. What's happened?"

"Oh Rod!" She burst into tears. "He heard about you and that it was Mingo who set you up. He was heartbroken. Mom said he just fell out of bed at about three in the morning. She called the ambulance and he's hanging in there, but he needs brain surgery and it doesn't look good."

Rod drove straight to the office of a lawyer he knew. The lawyer helped him turn himself in. Rod didn't care anymore about how many years he'd serve. He just needed to be allowed to visit his dad. Miraculously, the police agreed to let him go the day before his dad's brain surgery.

As Rod stood over the hospital bed crying, his dad grabbed his wrist and gripped it with amazing strength.

"Son, everything is going to be all right," he gasped weakly.

Rod knew he was on his way to the penitentiary for many years and that his dad would be dead soon. He couldn't understand what his father was trying to say.

"What do you mean, Dad?" he asked.

"Son, I just saw Jesus."

Rod's dad had never been much of a religious man, but Rod had always known he believed in Jesus Christ. Yet this was too much. Too strange.

"What, Dad?"

"He walked in and stood at the end of my bed. He said, 'You're going to come home, but I'm going to take care of your family.'"

Rod remembers being totally "freaked out" by his dad's bizarre words. He quickly changed the subject, remembering what it was like to be helpless in a hospital bed and hoping to alleviate some of his dad's fears. When he left his dad's side, he all but attacked the nurses' station.

"I want to know exactly what you've got my dad on," he demanded. "How many drugs are you giving him?"

"Oh, no, Mr. Anderson, he's not on anything," the nurse on duty responded. "We can't give him anything because of the surgery tomorrow. He's totally lucid."

Rod left, mystified about his dad's words. His dad went in for brain surgery and was slightly recovered two mornings later. He could not speak, but he could write messages, and he pressed a note into Rod's hand that read, "Take care of Mom."

Rod wept as his dad died.

When the hearing on his drug charges came up, he was sent to a twelve-man cell that was holding twenty-eight. He couldn't imagine how he would fulfill his dad's wishes when he'd be locked up for over twenty years. He understood they would automatically deny parole on his first three opportunities, so the first time he'd be in a parole hearing would be in the year 2003. It was only 1976.

While waiting in the crowded cell, Rod was told he had a visitor who would see him in the bail-bondsman's booth. "Hi, I'm Tom Alexander," said a nice-looking man. "I'm here to talk to you about Jesus."

"I've heard about Him," Rod said, thinking only of his father.

Tom gave Rod a gospel message for about twenty minutes, then led him to Christ right there. He parted with the words, "Greater is He that is in you, than he that is in the world." (See 1 John 4:4.) Rod laughed inwardly at the strange words. He went back to the cell, wondering what that was all about.

A few weeks later, Rod was allowed bail and released. He arrived a few weeks after that at his final court appearance, carrying a brown paper bag with three pairs of underwear, his toothbrush, and some toothpaste. He was ready for Chino State Prison, which would be the first stop in the next leg of his continuing prison career.

The sheriff who was so determined to see Rod behind bars was sitting with the detectives on the left. Rod was on the right with his attorney.

"Your honor, we want to bring up these charges, along with the drug running into Mexico, the airplanes, the profiteering...."

Rod listened incredulously to the long list of crimes they were pinning on him. He'd done some bad stuff, but they were giving him way too much credit. Suddenly he heard a voice from the back.

"Your Honor, I'm from Teen Challenge, and we're interested in this young man."

The judge's gavel cracked down. "Yes, I know who you are. Let's proceed."

Rod didn't know who he was, though, and swiveled to see Tom Alexander, the man in the bail-bondsman's booth who had prayed with him. Tom flashed Rod a big smile, and Rod remembered the strange words, "Greater is He that is in me, than he that is in the world."

Soon the judge was ready to pronounce sentence. He suddenly rapped his gavel and said, "I don't know why I'm doing this, but I'm sentencing you to nine months with Teen Challenge."

The sheriff leaped across the room and tried to grab Rod over the table. The bailiff jumped to stop him as the courtroom disintegrated into wild disorder. In the uproar, the judge's voice could be heard as his gavel continued rapping loudly, "If Mr. Anderson makes just one mistake, he goes back to prison for the maximum sentence of fifteen years to life."

The bailiff cleared everyone from the courtroom. The judge stood and stepped down to the back door, where he disappeared with a few law clerks and the district attorney, who was right behind him. Rod's attorney snapped shut his briefcase, shook hands with Rod, and walked out the back.

Rod sat alone in the empty courtroom with his brown paper bag of clean underwear sitting on the table in front of him.

Suddenly the back door opened and he heard Tom Alexander's voice again. "Come on, Rod, didn't I tell you that greater is He that is in you now, than he that is in the world?"

Rod rode with Tom to the Teen Challenge house that would now be his home. As they entered, he saw a group of eight people in a circle holding hands, praying. He realized they were praying for him, and that they'd been praying all morning.

At the Teen Challenge house, Rod excelled in their Bible studies. Soon, he began explaining to others the truths and principles he was learning in such a clear, cohesive way that the leaders encouraged him to pursue Bible training. A year later, Rod left Teen Challenge for Bible college in Tulsa, then went back to California to travel with a prison ministry for a few years. As his ability to teach the Bible increased, he started getting invitations to speak. Finally he was invited to join a Bible-college-planting organization where he could travel the world to build Bible schools.

While in Tulsa, Rod had the most startling revelation of his life. The weight of guilt from being responsible for his dad's stroke and death had never left him. He prayed, fasted, and repented, but to no avail. He couldn't be a good enough son or brother to make it up to his mother and sisters. He couldn't do enough good deeds as a Christian to outweigh the despicable behavior of his youth.

As he sat in his car one day, waiting for the doors to open at a Bible class, it suddenly occurred to him that nothing was ever going to change. Unless he made a decision otherwise, he was going to feel like a victim all his life and suffer the unrelenting weight of guilt and self-pity. Seeing clearly what had been so clouded for months, he started talking to himself.

"I'm the one," he said. "I'm the one who's going to have to change, to accept responsibility for my life. I can't allow the past to dictate my future. God's forgiveness has never changed. I've got to get it and go forward."

At that moment he made a conscientious choice to appropriate God's forgiveness and forgive himself daily. As he bathed himself in forgiveness, he changed inside. And as he changed internally, his future opened up before him.

For fifteen years, Rod has ministered in a Bible school in London. He and his British wife, Julie, are leaders in the English part of the great intercessory prayer movement that is now sweeping the world.

❖

Until the day Rod realized that "change is not change until it is change," he could not grow beyond his mind-set. Others have heard that saying, made a placard of it, and placed it on their office wall, in their bedroom, and on their bathroom mirror. But Rod put it in his heart. He was committed to it. He would change. Rod realized that not to forgive himself for something which God forgave was to make himself more important than God. If God could forgive, Rod could forgive.

No longer would he let his past victimize him, nor would he be a victim of the guilt it brought. Forgiveness was sought, given, and daily maintained by God's grace through faith in Christ. Rod was free.

Rod learned in doctrine and practice that what man covers, God will uncover; and what man uncovers, God will cover. (See Proverbs 25:2.) In the course of maturing in Christ, he needed courage to face his past, to uncover the guilt rather than continue to cover it. His guilt had led to poor self-esteem, which caused him to apologize constantly for his authority in teaching God's truths. His past eroded his present and troubled his future.

The devil is not only a tempter, but an accuser. He accuses God to men and men to God. When Satan cannot get a man through temptation, he'll try to bring him down through accusation. Oppression is often a characteristic of Satan's accusations. God forgives and releases. Satan never forgives and ever holds against men the things that through guilt will hold them back. The glory of God is that He rendered Satan's power null and void through Christ's death on the cross. He triumphed over Satan openly and causes us to do the same when we take all to the cross.

Victimized in his youth by those he ran with, Rod had developed a victim's mentality. The victim's mind-set is somewhat like "Murphy's Law": Whatever will go wrong, will go wrong for me. With this way of thinking, Rod had a problem allowing God to raise him to new levels in marriage and in ministry. For example, when God gave him a beautiful, British-proper, God-fearing wife, it was almost too much for him to accept. He had to learn that his wife and his teaching ability were supernatural gifts of God's grace and they did not depend on his performance.

Rod's story is not ended. It has an unusual twist. Of all the places for God to place a man with his background, he wound up in London, England, where he founded a Bible training center just blocks away from the House of Lords. He recently wrote, "Probably the greatest truth I've had to realize is that if change in my life was going to come, it was going to come from ME, not someone else. From the selfish destruction I went through with heroin addiction and prison, my greatest challenge was to dare to believe that God would take me from that background to a city like London and somehow be used of Him. To find myself today, ministering to some of the nation's spiritual leaders in the heart of Westminster, is mind-blowing! I'm continually humbled by what God has done so far, and yet I'm aware He hasn't even really started with me in many areas."

Just as God settled Rod's past 2,000 years ago at Calvary, He has settled your past. Give it to Him Who loved you enough to pay the price for your forgiveness and release from the sins of the past. Trust Him at this moment. Uncover it, and let God cover it with the cleansing blood of Jesus. *It is the glory of God to conceal a thing: but the honour of kings is to search out a matter* (Proverbs 25:2).

It is to your honor to admit it, and God's to cover it.

Join the ranks of the men who have had the courage to do it. Face your past by doing in the present what will become your future.

P R I N C I P L E S *for* COURAGEOUS MANHOOD

♦ WHAT MAN COVERS, GOD WILL UNCOVER; AND WHAT MAN UNCOVERS, GOD WILL COVER.

♦ CHANGE ISN'T CHANGE UNTIL IT IS CHANGE.

- NOT TO FORGIVE YOURSELF FOR SOMETHING WHICH GOD FORGAVE IS TO MAKE YOURSELF MORE IMPORTANT THAN GOD.

- WHEN SATAN CANNOT GET A MAN THROUGH TEMPTATION, HE'LL TRY TO BRING HIM DOWN THROUGH ACCUSATION.

FIVE

DON OSTROM

COURAGE TO LET GO

*Any death in Christ must be followed by
a resurrection or it is not a death in Christ.*

Everything within Don raged against what was happening to him. He'd pursued his dream, going to Bible college to become a minister, then launching off for the Philippines as a missionary with his wife, Marlene, and young son. He threw himself into the Philippine mission, starting a storefront church on the main street of bustling Davao City. His second son was born during their three happy years there and their church exploded to three hundred new converts. Only a tragedy could have brought them home, and it did.

Marlene's mother passed away shortly after they left for the Philippines. Two years later, she received the terrible news that her father and sister were killed in a private plane crash. Pregnant with their third child, busy with the first two sons, and grief-stricken at the loss of her father, Marlene raced home to the comfort of her friends and extended family. Three months later, Don was able to stabilize the work in the Philippines and join her in Seattle.

Don's plan was to settle the estate, sell the six nursing homes her father owned, then return as quickly as possible to the Philippines. But Marlene's dad had not signed his will, and settling the estate dragged on month after month. They had to maintain the nursing homes, stringing all the way from Seattle to Iowa. Don did what was necessary outwardly, but inwardly he deeply resented the death of his vision.

Longing to continue sharing the Gospel, Don scheduled himself into churches and traveled wherever he could get a meeting. That left Marlene, with their two toddlers and a brand new infant, to keep the house and manage the nursing homes. Unable to wing it alone, she hired a capable young man and spent hours with him every week pouring over the details, determined to keep her father's hard-earned businesses afloat.

Seeing his situation go from bad to worse, Don built up a resentment toward Marlene, which resulted in a full-blown jealousy toward the young man he viewed as a competitor for his wife's time. Their home life degenerated as Don vented his frustration and anger by sniping at Marlene, every word a potent weapon to destroy her.

"This is such a bad situation," he confided in an evangelist whom he entertained while the man spoke in a series of meetings at their church. "I just can't give up God's call on my life to operate this business. And Marlene is spending all her time with this other man, not even thinking of me and my ministry."

They talked over the course of a few days until the evangelist had heard and seen enough.

"Don," he said, "I think God has a message for you."

Eager to hear himself justified by a prophecy from his friend, Don listened attentively.

"He wants you to get off your butt and manage those businesses. So stand up and be a man. Take charge!"

Shocked as much at the man's language as his message, Don couldn't believe it could possibly be from God. But it jolted him into thinking in a different direction, and Don couldn't stop the man's words from ringing in his ears. In frustration, he went to his knees and asked God if he was a preacher or a businessman. The Lord spoke to him gently, reassuring him that it didn't matter what he called himself, so long as he did the Lord's will.

Don knew that he was wrong. The evangelist was right. Marlene had had enough. For them to prosper in life, Don was going to have to bury his dream of being a missionary.

The process was agonizing as Don gave up everything he loved. He learned to sit behind a desk crunching numbers, creating policies, wrestling with profit and loss statements, and interviewing employees.

About this time, Don started attending meetings held by Full Gospel Businessmen's Fellowship in his area. There, the stories of businessmen who had worked in ministry, even gone out on missions, allayed Don's fears of being stuck in business and gave him new hope.

Having been on the mission field himself, Don was well aware of the amount of money it would take to get churches planted and evangelism accomplished in the Philippines. He quickly realized that if he'd do what the evangelist said — stand up, be a man, and manage those businesses well — he could have the best of both worlds, financing missions as well as going on short mission trips himself.

Don returned to the Philippine church he started during the first year of his business. He has been able to make time available every year to spend at least two or three weeks with the people he had counted on living with forever.

Don didn't approach the business nonchalantly, but threw himself into it as he once had the mission. The six homes were too geographically diverse to manage efficiently, so when the estate finally settled, Don sold off the Iowa homes and reinvested in building up the homes in Washington State. He realized his most valuable asset was the good managers he had, and he started rewarding them with a new Cadillac every two years, cash bonuses, and vacation incentives for maintaining high standards of nursing care and good profits. The managers thrived under Don's liberal spirit. It soon became Don's way of keeping loyal administrators, and everyone has benefited as a result.

Step by step, Don was creating a tremendous cash flow to invest in missions. In time, he found his ministry wouldn't be limited to the Philippines. Through Full Gospel Businessmen's, he started traveling and ministering in other nations. Soon he and Marlene had a worldwide family of friends and ministry associates who helped fulfill and enrich their lives in ways they never imagined. Once Don let go of the smaller dream, God gave him the greater.

Don and Marlene have four sons, but it is their second, born on the mission field, who has followed Don into the business. Together, they have built what are now known as convalescent centers, assisted living homes, and retirement complexes that provide tremendous benefit to the communities they serve. The profits have enriched tens, even hundreds, of mission fields.

In the last twenty years, Don has ministered in sixty-two countries. He has never missed a year in the Philippines, and the little church he started has now spawned over 400 sister churches throughout that region. Keeping themselves young and fit, Don and Marlene expect many more productive years ahead.

⬦

If you look for the supernatural only in the spectacular, you will miss the Holy Spirit.

That is the singular reason too many neither know nor understand the ministry of the Holy Spirit in personal life. He is at work twenty-four hours a day in the lives of those who have received Christ Jesus as Savior and Lord.

At first glance, there is nothing unusual, unique, or rare about Don. However, with time and relationship you begin to find a rare jewel of human character combined with an unusual capacity of love, grace, and especially faith.

It took all of that to take him from the primitive missionary work in the Philippine Islands thirty-six years ago to an executive with incredible tenacity and moral strength. Even today, after all the years have gone by, there are still little earmarks of an earlier day begun in poverty and with a passion for God.

Nothing spectacular about him, but a life lived being led by the Spirit of God has made him a man among men, respected and admired.

At that missionary church he started decades ago in the Philippines, which has become 400 churches strong and where he returns annually to preach, they call him "Papa Ostrom."

His dream took him to forsake all and live and minister full-time on that island. Taking up his father-in-law's business, he had to die to his dream and heart's desire. But it is a truth we can depend on, that any death in Christ must be followed by a resurrection, or it is not a death in Christ.

All true joy is born out of sorrow. It was the death of a dream that grieved Don at first, but sorrow at giving up his dream in the islands was swallowed up by the joy of having more than he ever dreamed possible. Trying to hold on to the "little" at the expense of the "much" would have been a terrible disaster. It was a hard lesson to go from a non-profit organization to running a business that had to show a profit. Don had to learn to prosper in running the business. Without prospering there would be no growth.

It was necessary for Don to change the negative doctrine learned in his youth to give opportunity for prospering and profiting. His faith had to expand so his business could. The byproduct of expanded faith in business was the expansion in him, his marriage, and ministry.

Rather than ministering on one tiny island, Don began a work, sustained it, and in the ensuing years ministered around the world. Trips sponsored by the profit-making business funded the nonprofit ministry.

In addition, Don has had the great privilege of being friends and partners, with some of the greatest leaders in Christianity today. His and Marlene's life has not been spectacular in some ways, but it has been supernaturally led by the Holy Spirit. It took courage for him to give up his dream, but the faith he gained in exchange has been more than enough.

Once he solved his identity crisis — that he could be both a businessman and a missionary, so long as he identified himself first and foremost with Jesus Christ — then he was able to let go of his own dream and receive God's bigger dream. Tested, tried, and proven, Don is a man of courageous manhood.

Just ask his sons — or his wife.

P R I N C I P L E S *for* **COURAGEOUS MANHOOD**

- ♦ IF YOU LOOK FOR THE SUPERNATURAL ONLY IN THE SPECTACULAR, YOU WILL MISS THE HOLY SPIRIT.

- ♦ ANY DEATH IN CHRIST MUST BE FOLLOWED BY A RESURRECTION, OR IT IS NOT A DEATH IN CHRIST.

- ♦ ALL TRUE JOY IS BORN OUT OF SORROW.

- ♦ TRYING TO HOLD ON TO THE "LITTLE" AT THE EXPENSE OF THE "MUCH" IS A DISASTER.

SIX

ROBERT K.

COURAGE TO
ADMIT NEED

Men pray for victory, but God gives wisdom for
a strategy. It's the strategy that leads to the victory.

Robert didn't get it. Everyone else who was prayed for seemed to be instantly delivered from all their problems. Here he was, at his umpteenth Christian convention, still hung over from using drugs the night before. Why couldn't he just kick the habit like everyone else?

Born the first generation American of Russian immigrants, Robert had a pretty ideal family life. He was raised in good Southern California suburbs after his family earned enough to move away from the sprawling Los Angeles city that had so eagerly adopted their "different" culture. As a slightly overweight kid, he decided early that he had to work to fit in with the crowd. Finding himself in the "cool" crowd in eighth grade, he got high to gain their acceptance.

As a senior in high school, he got in on the "Jesus Movement," but doesn't remember if he made a real commitment or not. He repeated the sinner's prayer, but by that time he could not stay sober. Nevertheless, even though Robert could not surrender his addictions for God, God did not surrender Robert to his addictions.

Robert had a series of arrests for drug dealing that dogged his teens and twenties. Dealing kilos of cocaine to people, he would tell them, "This really isn't your answer, you know. Jesus is the only answer." A few actually got saved, and one of Robert's converts is serving the Lord today. Robert always felt better talking about Jesus, drugs or not, and he always tithed — even off his drug money. He gave in cash.

At a men's meeting in 1984, when he responded to another altar call, the preacher pointed to his friend who brought him and said, "This guy's got something going. Keep your eye on him."

Robert remembers those words. He knew he had something going, but he just couldn't get it going in the right direction. The following year, Robert went to hear the same man. He went outside during the break and, after lighting a joint, did something he'd never done before. He snuffed it out and slipped back into the crowded room to sit on the back row.

"You know we're men, so let's talk like men," the preacher said. "The Bible says that a double-minded man is unstable in SOME of his ways."

A few in the audience called out, "ALL!"

The preacher repeated, "A double-minded man is unstable in SOME of his ways."

This time they called out in unison, "ALL!"

"Is that what that says?" the preacher asked, and the men yelled, "YES!"

"So if a double-minded man is unstable in ALL his ways, that means he's got one leg on one side of the fence, and the other leg on the other side, and if he falls, you know what that's going to feel like!"

The men groaned in unison, but the words cut through Robert. It was so simple. He realized he had never really made up his mind. He left the meeting and soon served a jail sentence at the county facility, fully intending to go through the program and become single-minded, but he started using cocaine in jail and lasted only six weeks after his release. His habit ran his life.

He had wanted to enter a twelve-step program, but it worried him that he couldn't just be a single-minded Christian and have the desire for drugs taken out of his life. He wanted a "magical" solution that he'd seen God give other men.

One day Robert left a hotel room looking for hope and ended up at his parole officer's. The shame, embarrassment, and difficulty of yet another parole violation had brought him to a new low point. "Pitiful, incomprehensible demoralization," he called it.

The "double-minded man" was still in his head. After joining a drug rehabilitation program, he experienced some victory in his life and started building a real relationship with God. But he felt guilty, even though he was clean, because he depended on the support groups, not just God. When the next men's meeting came around, he again slipped into a back seat and caught that the preacher's theme was "wisdom."

"You pray for victory, but God gives you wisdom," the preacher said. "With the wisdom, you develop a strategy, and that leads you to your victory."

Robert thought about the twelve-step program he'd felt so guilty about — how he'd believed he was a failure for needing support. He'd never accepted the support wholeheartedly as a means to get out of the degrading lifestyle he'd created for himself. Once again, he walked to the altar.

"Do you mean it this time?" the preacher asked, pointing to him. Robert nodded quietly.

Immediately he joined a twelve-step program, and this time he made a lasting commitment. The support group was his strategy for victory. Although his deliverance was not instantaneous, it was nonetheless a miracle. "If I keep my strategy," he told the Lord daily, "I know You'll give me the victory!"

Robert has lost the "baby fat" he carried for thirty-five years, shedding sixty pounds that have stayed off. He's been sober since 1986, has married a beautiful Christian woman, just bought a new home, and adopted a beautiful baby boy to carry on his Russian name. The judge had tears in his eyes when he finalized Robert's adoption papers because of the change in Robert's life. "This one means a lot to me," he told Robert privately in chambers. "We don't give babies to scumbags."

Many of Robert's friends are dead. Some are in jail. A few are sober.

The biggest thing to Robert is that he stopped looking for the "big high." He has started to find his greatest pleasures in the small things — rolling around on the floor with his baby boy, or sitting on the pier at sunset talking to a friend.

Raised in Southern California in a fairly well-to-do family, Robert had a normal upbringing, until wanting to be accepted by his peers caused him to do things that almost ruined his life. Drugs always seem to provide pleasure, relief, and release from the pressures of life, only to cause pressures from which there is no relief or release.

Robert even thought a goal of being a drug dealer would be a worthy occupation, providing for himself while providing for others. To support the habit adds an additional burden — oppressive in its demands, coercive to fulfill its appetite, with an obligation to satisfy. But there is no satisfaction, only a momentary appeasement.

Robert struggled until it dawned on him that he needed help from sources beyond his own. Realizing he would never get help from the places that caused the problem, he turned to people he had formerly discounted as weird and off-the-wall in their thinking and way of living. He listened to them tell of the power of God, how Jesus Christ saves from the power of Satan, sin, and self. He decided to go with them to hear what was happening.

He was still foggy from the night before when he walked into that first meeting. Barely able to stay, he would leave intermittently, only to go back inside, determined to hear a word of encouragement or a formula to get rid of the habit. What he heard was not what he wanted to hear, so he left.

The next time, he returned with a desire to ask for help. Asking for help was one of the hardest things he could imagine. It meant he was not man enough to handle it by himself. He was failing. It impugned his masculinity. Pride had to give way to humility. That is the hardest thing for a man to do — to admit he's wrong and needs help.

Robert's need became greater than his pride. Something had to be done.

When the meeting was ending and a call was made for those who needed prayer to go forward, he walked to the front. When it was over, nothing had happened. He wanted the consequences to be gone, but not his sin. That mentality thrives in those who want to continue to live a licentious lifestyle, but want others to pay for their hospitalization. They want pleasure without penalty. They want to violate the laws of health without pain or plague — having their cake and eating it too.

Human sorrow wants to get rid of the consequences; godly sorrow wants to be rid of the sin.

Robert called on God, repented of his sin, and confessed Jesus as his Savior. He believed unto life eternal, but he still couldn't kick the habit. He had been prayed for, men of God had laid hands on him, and still the habit would not let go. He blamed himself for his failure. People suggested Alcoholics Anonymous and Narcotics Anonymous, but he refused to go. He believed it would be an admission of failure in faith, an accusation against God's character that He would not take the addiction from him.

Robert had been an audacious man while taking drugs and dealing them. Sentenced to jail for the sale of drugs, he stood in a men's meeting the night before he was to go and told them all he would be a "missionary in jail." When released, he returned to our men's meeting at the first opportunity. It was there he heard the truth that would start the process of setting him totally free from drugs. The truth was simply four words: Wisdom. Strategy. Victory. Glory.

Victory is a defeat over an enemy or an opponent. It means to win in a fight against an adversary. For Christians it is used as a word for salvation, healing, financial prosperity, or any kind of release or deliverance from an adversary. Adversaries in life can be diseases, habits, thought patterns, appetites, people, or sin and Satan. In religious "slanguage" when someone says, "I have the victory," it could mean a variety of good things. It could mean that a habit in life was broken, or anger and ill will toward someone was overcome by God's grace. It could just be sensing God's righteousness abiding in their spirit, or a migraine headache that troubled them is gone. For Robert, victory meant one thing: His drug habit was overcome and he was "clean."

In any war, the strategy is more important than the manpower. If you look only at manpower, victories could be won by a headcount. It's the strategy that leads to the victory. Winning strategies are developed by wisdom. *Wisdom is the principal thing; therefore get wisdom: and with all thy getting get understanding* (Proverbs 4:7).

So when someone wants victory, it needs to start with wisdom. God is a miracle-worker, not a magician. Some men pray for money and expect a check to float out of heaven. It won't happen. Men want victory, but they need wisdom to gain a strategy that will lead them to the victory.

The glory is in victory, not in defeat, nor in a truce. In World War II, America won a victory, but in the Vietnam war the country settled for a truce. The difference between the two is shown in how they treated the returning soldiers from each conflict. In the first, they were treated as heroes. In the second, they were regarded almost as villains. The glory was in the victory, but never in the truce.

Robert could have settled for a truce and could still be battling his addiction, finding ways to justify or excuse it, living in misery from its bondage. But when he heard the truth, he wanted to settle for nothing less than a victory over his obsession. His strategy was to join a support group. The prospect of baring his soul to others, actually being confronted by them, was terrifying. His audacity was a form of courage during the addiction, and that courage came to the fore again — not to find ways of getting and selling drugs, but to get rid of them.

Robert is still clean today. He has the victory! And he's living in the glory. The glory of the simple things is one of the grander experiences in life. Having a wife who loves him, being clean and sober, watching his son grow up — simple, but marvelous!

God's wisdom gave him a strategy, the strategy enabled him to obtain a victory, and the victory brought him glory. *But we all, with open face beholding as in a glass the glory of the Lord, are changed into the same image from glory to glory, even as by the Spirit of the Lord* (2 Corinthians 3:18).

God's purpose in a man's life is to see him changed from glory to glory by becoming more Christlike. Faith in Christ is the beginning of an adventure, and it's an ongoing pleasure to be changed from glory to glory by winning victory after victory. The change that takes you to the next level gives a greater sense of exhilaration than standing on the top of Mount Everest. There is far more satisfaction in a daily empowerment over temptation than a momentary gratification from the ecstasy of lust.

Courage must be added to faith to enjoy the glory, and the supremacy of facing your demons and overcoming them makes a champion of any man. Enjoying the glory of being a champion, winning the victory, is life's greatest accomplishment.

The incredible fullness of the stature of really mature manhood has no equal.

One may wonder why God didn't deliver Robert at the altar, as has happened to so many thousands of others. In the same way, one might wonder why one convicted felon is released from prison after receiving Christ, and another is left in jail for decades. The answer is: God's touch is constant, but His methods are instant. God's touch remains the same, changeless throughout eternity, but the methods He employs change with each individual. When Jesus healed the sick, the outcome was the same, but the method was always different. The touch was a constant, the method was only for the instant.

Today, to tell his story, Robert uses the tradition of anonymity he learned from the twelve-step groups by using only his last initial. There is no shame in it, only the glory of victory.

Robert, you found your God-given strategy and followed it to victory. We salute you! Live long and live well in Christ.

PRINCIPLES *for* COURAGEOUS MANHOOD

♦ THE HARDEST THING FOR A MAN TO DO IS TO ADMIT HE'S WRONG AND NEEDS HELP.

- HUMAN SORROW WANTS TO GET RID OF THE CONSEQUENCES; GODLY SORROW WANTS TO BE RID OF THE SIN.

- YOU PRAY FOR VICTORY, BUT GOD GIVES YOU WISDOM FOR A STRATEGY. THE STRATEGY LEADS TO THE VICTORY THAT RESULTS IN GLORY.

- THERE IS FAR MORE SATISFACTION IN A DAILY EMPOWERMENT OVER TEMPTATION THAN A MOMENTARY GRATIFICATION FROM THE ECSTASY OF LUST.

- GOD'S TOUCH IS CONSTANT, BUT HIS METHODS ARE INSTANT.

SEVEN

ALLEN LEGIER

COURAGE TO
FORGIVE

Forgiveness opens; unforgiveness closes.
Forgiveness releases; unforgiveness binds.

Allen and his wife Donna lived on an acreage in Tahlequah, Oklahoma, the capitol of the Cherokee nation, with their three children, the oldest of which was Allen Jr. Both transplanted from Louisiana, they settled comfortably into rural life and Donna home-schooled the children while Allen worked as a surgical nurse in the Indian hospital.

Occasionally, Allen would get a call at work that one of Donna's migraines had flared up. The migraines were so fierce, she said it felt like the pain was dragging her down on her left side and she'd have to lay down. Allen would hurry home to watch the children while she slept it off. Donna hadn't had a headache for almost two years when he received a shocking call from her. She was driving to Louisiana for a brief visit and her left leg had gone completely numb.

When Donna returned, Allen first took her blood pressure, which appeared normal. But when he told her to try to stomp the floor as hard as she could and her left leg barely grazed the carpet, he was alarmed. He took her to the hospital the next day. The doctor ordered an MRI scan of Donna's brain. The radiologist left for dinner, so Allen stood at the controls and viewed the thirty scans of the brain, with Donna looking over his shoulder. He saw it clearly. A massive tumor covering a huge portion of her brain. He nervously switched images and saw it again. Glancing at Donna, it was obvious to him she didn't know what she was looking at.

He drove home morosely, keeping the bad news from his wife and preparing himself to believe for the best. Two days later the doctor sent them to a neurosurgeon, who broke the news to Donna. That night Allen and Donna told the children that she was seriously ill, and Allen led the family in a prayer of faith for divine intervention.

That week Allen and Donna flew to the Mayo Clinic for the top medical help in the U.S. After two brain surgeries, doctors shook their heads at Allen, admitting there was nothing they could do. They gave her six months to live, but she died in less than a month.

Allen went back home to break the news to his children — twelve, ten, and eight years old — kids who believed God would heal their mother. They were shocked. As the oldest, Allen Jr. felt the loss the greatest. Allen arranged services at their local church, with all three children standing with him at the coffin to shake hands with the many mourners — most of whom were strangers to them. Then Allen and the children flew with the coffin to Louisiana, where another service preceded Donna's burial. More people. More handshakes. His children wide-eyed in disbelief at the strange things happening to them. Allen Jr. valiantly setting a good example of strength for his little sisters.

The many mourners, memorial services, strange airports, and hospital waiting areas drained the children emotionally and physically. When Allen finally got them home they retreated to their bedrooms in stunned exhaustion. But Allen couldn't go back to his. He drug the mattress from his and Donna's room to the living room floor and there started a prayer meeting. Miserable, numb, feeling detached from the world, God became Allen's closest friend. God's presence filled the living room that first night, and many nights after.

Allen found himself awaking at three in the morning for nights on end, praying and pacing as God's presence enveloped him. Allen would leave for work after three hours of sleep and feel the presence of God sustain him physically. It was as if others should be able to see physically that Allen was not Allen anymore — he'd been filled with God's Spirit and that's all there was of him. His senses were heightened, his spirit more fully alive than ever. He couldn't even look at tabloid headlines in the grocery store without feeling a taint come over what was so holy and pure within him. He led his children in prayer and helped them grieve for their mother.

A month passed and Allen moved back into his own room. Slowly, the supernatural glow ebbed away and he fell into a normal routine. He had no signs of grief left. Then, months after the funeral, he met another beautiful woman.

"Did you see that blonde behind us?" Allen's father asked after church one Sunday.

"No," Allen said. He led praise and worship, but hadn't even noticed the new woman in their small church.

"Well, notice the next time!" his dad said.

The next week Allen saw her. Sweet-faced with a glowing smile, her presence lit up the pew where she sat.

"Who is she?" he asked the pastor immediately after service.

"Her name's Cheryl. She's new," the pastor answered.

"And?"

"What?"

"Is she married, divorced...?" Allen asked.

"She's been divorced about a year," the pastor answered.

Allen talked to Cheryl's mother next and a few weeks later invited Cheryl to attend a church conference in Tulsa with him. Up close, she proved to be as sweet, genuine, and beautiful as she was from afar. Allen prayed fervently about the relationship and six months later they married.

Cheryl left her job for Allen's house, bringing her two children, ages six and eight. The oldest was the same age as Allen's youngest. Being a trained speech pathologist, Cheryl knew how to handle kids. But within a month, Allen's two oldest decided Cheryl would not do for a mother. They went to war.

"Boo!" Allen Jr. screamed as Cheryl entered her dark bedroom. Cheryl jumped and shrieked, and Allen Jr. ran out laughing. When Allen scolded him, he said he intended it as a joke. But he did it often, and it was not funny to Cheryl. No matter how much Allen corrected or disciplined, nothing seemed to thwart Allen Jr.'s malicious pranks.

"AHHHHH!" Cheryl rocked the house screaming. Allen Jr. had wired 110 volts to his bedroom doorknob and sent an electric jolt through Cheryl's arm as she tried to enter his room. He told his dad he meant the trap for his little sisters, but Cheryl knew he was elated that she had been his victim.

Within six months Cheryl's sweet face was growing haggard. After a year, she knew she needed to work — somewhere outside the home and away from the kids. But she couldn't get far enough away. Their onslaught was unrelenting. For four long years Cheryl could do no right by her stepchildren. Allen was so concerned, he wondered often if he'd made a mistake. Was it all too much, too sudden for his kids? No amount of prayer, discipline, or counseling was changing the situation. Had he missed God?

When Allen Jr. was close to seventeen, Allen took him to a men's meeting. It was something Allen had been part of for years and he was excited to share it with his son. But nothing gave him an inkling of the next bomb that was to drop in their lives.

"If you don't forgive others, then God cannot forgive you," the preacher said to the men that day with simple clarity. "And Jesus taught, that whosoever sins we forgive, they are released. But whosoever sins we do not forgive, they are retained. (See John 20:23.) In other words, when you don't forgive, you retain that person's sins inside yourself."

Before the afternoon break, the preacher gave the crowd of men an opportunity to come to the front to repent of unforgiveness. Allen Jr. raced to the front. Allen followed his son, astonished, but thanking God that something was going on in his son's life.

"What's happening here?" the preacher asked, looking at Allen. Allen shrugged.

"What's going on, son?" he stooped over, asking Allen Jr. to his face. Unstoppable tears coursed down Allen Jr.'s face and he couldn't answer. "Come up here," the preacher said.

Allen Jr. stepped up on the platform where the preacher hugged him as he continued ministering to the others. When he released him, Allen, Jr.'s tears had almost stopped and the preacher asked him again what was happening inside.

"I forgive God," Allen Jr. said, crying again. "I forgive God for taking my mom. And I'm sorry I've been so mean to my stepmother."

Allen was standing in front of him. By this time, he and most of the men in the building were also crying. Everyone understood that God didn't need forgiveness, but Allen Jr. needed to forgive for his sake. His wrong thinking caused wrong conduct.

"Son," the preacher said, taking bills out of his pocket and pressing them into Allen Jr.'s hand, "If you're serious about this, then I want you to act like a man, and I want you to take your family out after church tomorrow. You choose the restaurant, you make the arrangements, and then you tell them what God did in your life today."

Allen Jr. shoved the bills in his pocket, hugged the preacher again, then stepped down into the arms of his father. They cried and hugged for a long time after the other men left for their break.

That night, Allen Jr. announced to his brothers and sisters that they'd be going to dinner the next day "on him." He called Cheryl's parents and asked them to join the family after Sunday services. When church was out, he ushered everyone into the restaurant, making a great show of telling them to order what they wanted because he was paying. Only scraps were left on a few plates when Allen Jr. spoke up from his place at the head of the table and said what he'd come to say.

"I want to tell you all what happened to me yesterday," he said confidently. "I forgave God because I thought he took away my mother. I didn't know that it was Him I was really mad at, but it was. Now I need to ask for forgiveness."

Allen Jr. turned to Cheryl and spoke to her directly. "It wasn't your fault and you've always tried to be there for me, but I was just mad, and I took it all out on you. I want to apologize to you for the way I've treated you ever since you married Dad, and from now on, you're my mom."

Cheryl's father could stand it no longer. Weeping, he stood up and walked over to give Allen Jr. a hug. By this time, the large party, in tears, had attracted the attention of other diners. Those sitting close enough were crying along with the family. One stranger rose, shook Cheryl's father's hand and said it was the most incredible scene he'd ever witnessed.

Next it was Allen Jr.'s turn. He rose from where he was seated, went to Cheryl's chair, and gave his mother a warm, welcome hug.

Allen says his son has not been the same since. Four years have passed and his son is preparing to leave college. But his greatest life's lessons have long since been indelibly imprinted on his life, and Allen has no worries of where God will lead him.

Cheryl and Allen are presently living with five teenagers in the house, but Allen is confident that God's love is able to cover any offense, any tragedy, and any difficulty. His love conquers all.

Everything God does is according to a pattern and based on a principle in His kingdom. Here is the pattern taught by Jesus in the parable of the prodigal (See Luke 15:11-24): Rebellion, ruin, repentance, reconciliation, and restoration. Repentance is the pivotal point between ruin and reconciliation.

Allen Jr's. rebellion, though directed against his new mother, was actually against God. Being mad at God is unnatural, but not abnormal. When he repented of his anger toward God and his resentment toward his new mother, the love of God was shed abroad in Allen Jr.'s heart. Repentance was the key to finding intimacy with God and then reconciliation to his new mother.

When Allen Jr. repented, he allowed the Holy Spirit to work in his heart to produce the ability to forgive. Then forgiveness opened the relationship that had been closed by unforgiveness.

In the principle of John 20:23, Jesus said, *Whose soever sins ye remit, they are remitted unto them; and whose soever sins ye retain, they are retained.* That means: Forgiveness opens; unforgiveness closes. Forgiveness releases; unforgiveness binds. Forgiveness freed Allen Jr. from anger toward God and made it possible for him to really accept his stepmother for the first time.

God is holy. Love is the manifestation of holiness, so God is love. The essence of love is found in grace, which is the ability to love when there is no basis for it other than the nature of the one who loves. Mercy is the gift of grace. The highest act of mercy is forgiveness.

Holy — love — grace — mercy — forgiveness. That means: Forgiveness is the visible expression of true holiness. The absence of forgiveness is evidence of failing in holiness.

Allen Jr. forgave, and God's love gave him a greater degree of holiness.

It was God's truth that opened the eyes of Allen Jr.'s understanding. But it was courage that caused him to walk forward in front of all the men in the hall. God didn't need to be forgiven, Allen Jr. did. God hadn't done any wrong, Allen Jr. had by venting his resentment at the loss of his mother.

"Good courage" is different than "courage." Many men exhibit courage to do wrong — rob a bank or pick a fight, as examples. Good courage is doing right at the expense of wanting to do wrong. Staying in his seat and refusing to admit his sin against his family would have been an act of the wrong kind of courage. Good courage was standing up like a man and admitting his wrong, with a desire to stop it and do right.

Once done, it was easy to follow it up at the restaurant, publicly asking his new mother to forgive him. To confess what Jesus Christ, by His Spirit, had done in his heart and life in front of everyone was manly.

Cheryl showed more than a mother's love in forgiving Allen Jr. She forgave with God's love. His love is unconditional, sacrificial, and redemptive.

Love covers a multitude of sins, covers them with forgiveness. Forgiveness brings healing where there is hurt, closeness where there is distance, and understanding where there has been enmity.

P R I N C I P L E S *for* COURAGEOUS MANHOOD

♦ IF YOU DON'T FORGIVE OTHERS, THEN GOD CANNOT FORGIVE YOU. WHEN YOU DON'T FORGIVE, YOU RETAIN THAT PERSON'S SINS INSIDE YOURSELF.

♦ EVERYTHING GOD DOES IS ACCORDING TO A PATTERN AND BASED ON A PRINCIPLE IN HIS KINGDOM.

♦ FORGIVENESS IS THE VISIBLE EXPRESSION OF TRUE HOLINESS.

♦ REPENTANCE IS THE PIVOTAL POINT BETWEEN RUIN AND RECONCILIATION.

♦ GOD'S LOVE IS UNCONDITIONAL, SACRIFICIAL, AND REDEMPTIVE.

♦ FORGIVENESS OPENS; UNFORGIVENESS CLOSES. FORGIVENESS RELEASES; UNFORGIVENESS BINDS.

RAYMOND T. MEZA

COURAGE TO
BE FAITHFUL

By being faithful in that which is another man's,
it qualifies you for that which is your own.

What do a post and a pillar have in common?

The same thing New Zealand, Mexico, Venezuela, Brazil, Canada, Germany, Poland, England, and the United States have in common.

The answer is Raymond Meza.

In 1947 a man named Homer G. Nickel founded a fence company. He sold cedar posts for building fences on large Texas ranches. Stocks of cedar posts were stacked everywhere in the small company yard, and over the years, as the company grew, the yard was expanded to accommodate the stacks.

The seven-year-old son of a Mexican immigrant who worked in the yard was given the job of picking up the nails that fell where the fence-building was done. The boy would walk around the yard pulling a rope with a magnet tied to the end. As he dragged the magnet, it would attract and pick up the nails. The workers did not pay much attention to the little boy who was walking around the yard.

Raymond learned in his early youth to let neither the insignificance nor the difficulty of a job deter him in his desire to succeed — whether at work, at school, on the city streets, or at home. No one could discourage him. He persevered to overcome whatever came at him. As a result, people gave him the jobs they didn't want, and each time he excelled and was promoted.

As he grew older, Raymond was allowed to stack posts in addition to picking up nails. He worked in loading, then eventually was given the position of foreman of the welding shop when he graduated from high school. After serving as a foreman, he finally took off his coveralls and became an accomplished salesman, leaving the yard for the office.

Raymond was so successful in sales, he was soon made Construction and Sales Manager. He began to export products to Canada, England, Mexico, Venezuela, Poland, and Brazil. Opening sales offices in those countries, he expanded the growth of the company exponentially. He established patterns of prompt delivery and customer satisfaction, giving rare face-to-face service. He also ensured they were a full-service fence company. Customers appreciated dealing with one company for construction, sales, distribution, delivery, post-hole drilling, and design consultation.

When Raymond heard of battery- and solar-powered electric wire fencing, he immediately saw the future potential. The leading supplier was in New Zealand, so he encouraged the owner, Homer's son Robert A. Nickel, to sign an exclusive distribution contract for the United States and Mexico with the New Zealand firm. They did, and today electric fencing is one of the essential commodities for the company.

At the end of five years as Sales Manager, seeing the company develop and grow under his stewardship, Raymond desired to buy it. Throughout his tenure, he had rigidly maintained his personal loyalty to Mr. Nickel and had remained ever diligent to make the company successful. He still points to Mr. Nickel as "the only boss I ever had."

Knowing every facet of the company from having worked at every position, he knew how it operated and what it took to make it successful. It was something he could do and really enjoy. So he decided to buy it. When he approached Mr. Nickel, he was amenable to the purchase, but then Raymond was unable to secure the funding. Without funding, there was no deal.

During Raymond's long climb to the top, his wife, Norma, helped support the family with her seamstress skills. A godly woman, she prayed for Raymond daily and engaged her prayer group in intercession for him. After twenty years of prayer for Raymond at the fence company, she started seeing God's answers.

When Raymond couldn't buy the company, for the first time in his life he began to realize he could not do it all himself. He needed help — not just to buy the company, but personally. The conviction grew within him that he needed something more than what he had. He had always attended church, but only to make his family happy and to give the right appearance. He would pray, but his prayers were centered on himself.

Then one Sunday he heard that his daughter had requested prayer for him in her Sunday school class. She had been asking her dad for money every Sunday. He didn't know it was because she wanted to sow offerings along with her prayers, praying to reap a harvest. She told a young evangelist visiting their church, "I want my dad to know Jesus."

Everyone joined in agreement with the little girl that he would be saved. The report touched Raymond's heart. It also touched the heart of the young preacher, who paid a house call to Raymond. Sitting in his living room, Raymond suddenly realized what he needed to do. In simple terms, he asked God to forgive him. He believed.

Raymond soon discovered a difference between just growing in favor with man and growing in favor with God and man. When God came first, the impossible became possible. What was bound was loosed. Where he had previously met stone walls, now there were none. His world changed when he changed.

Eager to grow beyond the Bible stories he'd heard all his life, Raymond went to a men's meeting with a friend. He almost wished he hadn't when he experienced that uncomfortable feeling of being seen right through. The man ministering told him everything wrong about himself, and in no uncertain terms told him he'd have to shape up. Raymond felt like he was the only man in the crowded room.

Raymond was especially convicted for the stinginess of what he threw into the offering plate each Sunday. He went home intent upon learning to tithe and give offerings. It was the last thing he wanted to do. Giving what had been so hard to earn was almost impossible. So deeply ingrained was his work ethic and fiscal responsibility, that he had to change his entire way of thinking to part with a dollar at church. But whatever Raymond sets his mind to, he does, and very quickly he turned things around financially, at home and in business, by putting God first.

Raymond was stunned when almost immediately after he started to give, the funding became available to buy the company. He had been ready to give up the dream just to follow God; but instead, God gave him his greatest desire. The local newspapers lauded him when the deal was known, writing about the boy who picked up nails and became the company owner. His friends, employees, customers, and family encouraged him, praising him for his faithfulness, perseverance, and honesty that had moved him into the top spot.

Now, thirty-three years from the day he first started work, Raymond has a multimillion dollar international company that is still growing.

And Raymond is still growing. Long accustomed to serving others, Raymond has a servant's heart. Serving his employer, supervisors, customers, family, and finally God has put him where he is today. Now he has begun to serve in a way far different from what he ever imagined.

Traveling to other countries and speaking in men's meetings, Raymond shares the truths, precepts, and principles that enabled him to grow to the place he is today. Thousands of men have heard his inspirational and instructional messages, giving them hope and confidence in Christ.

Raymond Meza is a pillar in his community, church, and family, yet he sells posts for a living. That is how the pillar and post have something in common. He is a common man living an uncommon life God's way.

What struck me about Raymond the first time I met him and heard his story was his willingness to be ordinary. He faced the position he was given with courage, which allowed him to accomplish extraordinary things in life.

Courage is defined by *Webster's New World College Dictionary* (© 1996) as, "the attitude of facing and dealing with anything recognized as dangerous, difficult, or painful, instead of drawing back from it; quality of being fearless or brave; valor." Raymond is the living epitome of this definition.

Thirty-three years after starting to pick up nails, the "little boy" became the boss of those still working in the yard. He let no menial task deter him, no difficulty of assignment discourage him, no hard work dissuade him from his desire to succeed.

Raymond unwittingly followed the principle that says, "The man who knows how will always have a job, but the man who knows why will always be his boss." He also followed the principle he had learned from his father: "To be promoted, work on yourself, not on others."

Based on these principles, his life followed a biblical pattern of which the Lord said, *And if ye have not been faithful in that which is another man's, who shall give you that which is your own?* (Luke 16:12) In other words, by being faithful in that which is another man's, it qualifies you for that which is your own.

By being faithful in his work at the fence company and loyal to its owner, Raymond had become qualified to have his own.

"Having been faithful with that which was another man's, I was given the opportunity to buy the company I pulled a nail magnet for as a child," he said to me recently. "I tried my best to buy this company through my own efforts. I was going through the motions of being a Christian — I attended church regularly, prayed and asked God to help ME buy this company.

"After attending that men's meeting, I began to tithe and give offerings — actually *giving* to God as I now understood it, instead of *tipping* God. I used to give a dollar and had a hard time letting go. Now I have no trouble doing it since I know it is the right thing to do. God was waiting for me to let go, because He already had it worked out.

"I have personally learned and experienced the truth that, 'maturity does not come with age, but with the acceptance of responsibility.'" Raymond has been willing to accept responsibility since he dragged that magnet at age seven. Today, his maturity is shown in the responsibility he's been given.

Thirty-three years after going to work for the company as a boy, he became the company owner. Less than a year after giving his life to Christ, he was able to do what had been unattainable before. Recently Raymond was named "Exporter of the Year" by his region's Small Business Administration. He is also the new Chairman of the Board for his city's Chamber of Commerce.

We applaud you and appreciate you, Raymond, for your courage to stand faithful.

P R I N C I P L E S *for* COURAGEOUS MANHOOD

♦ BY BEING FAITHFUL IN THAT WHICH IS ANOTHER MAN'S, IT QUALIFIES YOU FOR THAT WHICH IS YOUR OWN.

♦ THE MAN WHO KNOWS HOW WILL ALWAYS HAVE A JOB, BUT THE MAN WHO KNOWS WHY WILL ALWAYS BE HIS BOSS.

♦ WORK ON YOURSELF, NOT ON OTHERS, FOR YOUR PROMOTION.

♦ MATURITY DOES NOT COME WITH AGE BUT WITH THE ACCEPTANCE OF RESPONSIBILITY.

NINE

BEE MIDDLEBROOK

COURAGE TO
PERSEVERE

Perseverance will always outlast persecution.

"You leave us no choice, Bee. One!" The belt hit his back with a sting.

"Two!" The board crashed down on his legs.

"Three." The woman with the belt drew it across him again.

"Four," his mom called as her board hit him again on the legs. All three hundred "whacks" had to be given, plus extras if Bee cried or whimpered.

His mother's roommate, newly released from prison, gave most of the discipline. But it was physically demanding giving the 300-500 whacks he often deserved, so she enlisted his mom's help. Bee stood between the two of them, his blue eyes glazing over, keeping his mouth shut, as they counted off his whacks.

Bee had no other place to go. His father rejected him at birth because of the defect he was born with — a small left hand — and walked out on Bee's mother a few months later.

"What happened to your knees?" one of Bee's school teachers asked him one day. Bee was too ashamed to tell her he'd been forced to kneel on the old-fashioned heating grate at his mom's house until they bled. The teacher had already caught sight of the black and blue marks on his shoulders, back, arms, and legs, even though Bee always doubled his shirts and trousers to conceal them.

"Shall I report this?" she asked tenderly.

"No, please don't," Bee said, suddenly concerned for his mother's welfare and that of his own. He was the only person in the house who worked, and he couldn't think of any way for them to get by without him. "See, I'm the breadwinner and it won't stop what's happening anyway. They'll only send *me* away somewhere — to a juvenile home or something."

Convinced by the curious, grown-up little boy, the teacher dropped the issue, but allowed Bee to change into gym clothes in a separate room, to spare him embarrassment with the other kids. Bee wasn't accustomed to anyone sparing him embarrassment. Once when he was twelve, his mother and her roommate found his bed wet in the morning. It was the middle of summer, so they put two diapers together and dressed him in them — just the diapers — then sent him outdoors. All day, if he wasn't in view, they would call to the other kids to find him and bring him out of hiding.

Since he was ten years old, Bee awoke at midnight regularly to work the streets, then run an early morning paper route before school. After school he worked odd jobs until dinner, then slept until midnight. On the streets, he found errands he could run for husslers, drug dealers, and prostitutes, then learned how to augment his earnings with theft. He made enough money to keep his household in groceries, turning over his income to his mother.

"God's way is the family way," he heard at different times. He saw June and Ward Cleaver on television go to church on Sundays, and he dreamed of such a family and life.

When the opportunity came, Bee went to the meetings of a traveling healing preacher. His eyes widened as he saw people get up out of wheelchairs, and others fall under the power of God. After two days of waiting in line, he saw the man come his way. He lifted his small left hand. The man placed his hand on Bee's and prayed. Bee waited. Nothing happened. The preacher left him to continue down the endless line of people. Bee stood there alone, a strange little boy holding up his arm in a sea of people, waiting, not believing that after two days it was over without anything happening. Angry, Bee headed for the back door. He didn't cry. He never cried. But he couldn't get far enough away from the stabbing pain that now stung worse than any whacks. First his dad rejected him. Then his mom. And now God.

In high school he joined athletics, but at night he ran prostitutes. He joined a motorcycle club, where he found men willing to mentor him. At seventeen, his mom became furiously jealous about his friendship with another high school athlete. She bought Bee a suitcase at the Goodwill Store and said, "Get out of here." Within months, the motorcycle clubhouse became his home, the club his family, and he quickly moved up the ranks. Finally, he was accepted.

Bee married at twenty-six, and they had a baby boy. But the marriage faltered within months, forcing Bee to review his situation. He couldn't just divorce his wife, because she knew too much about his work in the club. All he could do was bury her. But he wanted to be able to say to his son one day, "I did everything I could," so his son wouldn't blame him later in life for growing up without a mom. Bee rehearsed the words in his mind, but they fell flat. In good conscience, he knew there was one more thing he had to try. He decided to move to a major neighboring city to find "God's way, the family way." If that failed, he could do what he needed to do.

Bee went to the city before his family to find carpentry work. While he was there, he looked up a youth pastor he knew.

"Can I see you?" Bee asked him over the telephone.

"Sure, Bee, why don't you come over for dinner tonight?"

Bee dined in the young family's kitchen, a room decorated in resplendent pink. The pastor's wife tried to appear unrattled when Bee showed up in his leathers, carrying his saddle bags, with his long beard, ponytail, and the rest of him in bad need of a wash. When the wife left to put her children to bed, Bee leaned close to the youth pastor.

"Is this a hussle?" he asked the young man.

"What?"

"This Jesus thing. Is it on the level?"

"Yes, Bee, it is!" the man said. "We can pray right here and you can see for yourself."

They discussed the Bible, Bee prayed a prayer, and then he left into the night to bring back his wife and son. Within days, his little family had moved into the pastor's house.

"You know, that kind of makes Linda nervous," the youth pastor told Bee, pointing to one of Bee's guns.

"What?" Bee asked.

"The guns," the youth pastor said.

"What? Don't you have guns?" Bee asked.

The youth pastor shook his head. Bee suddenly realized the house was wholly unarmed and unprepared, so he mounted a gun behind the door, kept one next to his bed on the fold-out couch, and left the house each night to sleep in the van with the dog and his gun, as was his habit. He felt good that he could do the naive young family a favor by protecting them and keeping watch. Linda later told Bee she was certain they were all going to die.

"You really need to return everything you've stolen," said the pastor during their first weeks together. Bee prayed with him and let his words settle in. A few days later he took back the possessions whose source he could remember — including his beloved Harley and truck. The rest he took to the church basement, almost filling it. When he cleaned house from everything stolen, the only thing Bee owned was a jean jacket his brother had given him and his colors. He kept the leathers and jeans he owned because no one would want them back anyway. It was not Bee's custom to wash clothes or bathe regularly.

"I called the police about the stuff in the church basement," the pastor said. "They came and picked it up, but they said they're going to arrest me for harboring a fugitive."

The pastor brought it up to Bee several times that week before Bee realized that the pastor didn't want to be arrested before Sunday service and that he was asking Bee to talk to the police himself.

Talk to the law! Talk? Bee and the pastor fasted and prayed for three days, then Bee went to the police station. The officer took out file after file and asked if Bee's goods were from those robberies. Bee helped him catalog as much as he could remember, then the officer closed his files, stood up, and said, "Thank you, you're free to go."

Free! Free? Bee was astounded. At church the next Sunday someone gave him some money, and within a month after moving to the city, he and his family moved into their own home. Strange, demonic things went on in their new home — the same things that had happened everywhere Bee lived. Bee was annoyed that the demons he'd once worshipped at a Satanic church continued to follow him. He invited the pastor over and they took oil around the house, anointing it and praying over every room.

The next day, the strange things stopped, but Bee's wife announced she was leaving. Bee wandered for a time, trying to get his wife back, trying to find some roots. He was asked to find another place to worship, which became a pattern. After attending a church a few times, people would ask him to attend elsewhere. He wore leather pants and carried saddle bags. He had long hair and a longer beard. He had dark, glassy eyes. He thought he had cleaned up, but he smelled.

Bee told new recruits in the motorcycle club, "You're after this, but you really need Jesus." Some listened and are still serving God today — outside the club. It hurt to leave the only family he knew, but he finally became an "inactive" member, only attending large parties and making an occasional appearance at the clubhouse. He drove trucks and worked construction, occasionally attending Bible studies with a sweet, God-fearing woman named Marlene.

Persevering by trying to understand the Bible on his own kept him from leaving God, but he couldn't connect with a church.

Just days away from getting custody of his son, he had to prove he had a job, but his Christian boss fired him. Bee had seen his son at his wife's apartment just days earlier with twenty hits of speed in his tiny hand. Bee couldn't contain the rage he felt for not being able to remove his son from such a situation. Facing rejection again, when he was trying so hard, moved him to swift action. He loaded his truck with dynamite and set out to blow up the man's business, but he stopped at Marlene's on the way and told her his plan.

"Oh, no you're not," she said defiantly. He spun around from her and marched to his truck. Before he could start it, he saw petite little Marlene standing in front of the truck.

"Get out of the way!" he yelled. She put her arms on her hips, making herself as big as she could, and glared at him.

"GET OUT OF THE WAY!" he roared, and started his engine. She didn't move. He flung open his door and jumped out of the truck, physically picking Marlene up and moving her onto the lawn. But when he got back in the cab, she was standing in front of his truck again. Her perseverance paid off. After four or five times, watching Marlene's little feet storm back to the truck, Bee's anger dissolved into laughter, and the emotion of the moment turned into an admiration for Marlene that eventually led to love and an "odd couple" marriage.

Through Marlene, Bee started listening to tapes which helped him make sense out of the Bible. He repented for the way he had acted. He repented for the way he was. He received instruction from others, and his exterior began to change. His manners, mannerisms, and looks were completely altered. His eyes cleared, so that even his eye color changed.

Bee repented to his mother, his son, and finally to his father for the anger he felt toward them and for how his father had let them down. His parents continue to reject him, but in 1997, his son became a Christian.

Today Bee is as hooked into men's ministry as he once was into the motorcycle club. He has traveled internationally, telling bits of his story. He is helping to develop a "truckers church" at a local truck stop. And he and Marlene now live much like June and Ward, attending church each Sunday, but with a fullness and wealth of life that Bee never knew existed — not even on television.

❧

Other men who experienced difficult childhoods die, are eaten up with bitterness, spend life in prison, or become old misanthropes. Bee became a man of God because of his perseverance. His life proves the truth that perseverance will always outlast persecution.

I was not prepared for my initial meeting with Bee. The leather clothes, long pony-tailed gray hair, disfigured hand, long beard, tattoos covering his body, and even his gait as he walked. Neither was I primed or ready to hear all he had to say.

But after sitting with him, talking to him, and praying with him, I found him to be one of the most open, honest, good spirited, and truthful men I have ever met. The stories he tells concerning his life prior to his rebirth in Christ, and even after, are incredible.

As the Apostle Paul used his life before he met Christ on the Damascus Road as a testimony to the power of God's presence, so Bee uses his for the glory of God. He does not regale people with sordid tales for shock value, but as naturally as breathing he tells what he went through to get where he is by faith.

Bee needed the courage of perseverance just to survive, much less live. On a trip to Nicaragua, the men who were rebels before Christ gravitated to Bee as their hero. They bonded in their love for God and His saving grace.

Bee needed courage to break with his covenant partners in crime and overcome the fear of their revenge. Living night and day with the realization they could be just outside his door at any moment was far more difficult than being with them, knowing they were his protection.

Bee needed courage added to his faith to overcome the evil one. Converted from a life of submitting to evil to a life of submitting to righteousness was not easy. What is submitted to in life grows stronger, while what is resisted grows weaker. Eventually Bee grew comfortable with the truth that submitting to the Lord gives ability to resist the devil. His mind and heart had been the devil's playground. Being dispossessed, Satan afflicted and tormented him mentally, emotionally, and socially.

These things I have spoken unto you, that in me ye might have peace. In the world ye shall have tribulation: but be of good cheer [courage]; *I have overcome the world* (John 16:33).

Bee persevered in repentance, missing the mark by far, but going back to the cross on his knees in true heartfelt repentance. Godly sorrow gripped his heart — not human sorrow that is only sorrow for the consequences of sin, but a sorrow for sin. Nor is it a one-time attempt at asking God for forgiveness, but a continuing earnest seeking after God with a desire to be Christlike.

The difference between Bee and others to whom he ministered was that when the consequences were alleviated, so was their need for God. In prison, it is called "jailhouse religion." It's as phony as a three-dollar bill — hypocrites. And the biggest hypocrite of all, is the man who believes in his heart in God, but won't confess it because he doesn't want to be identified publicly with Jesus Christ. Not so with Bee. He believed, and once he believed he persevered until God changed him.

There are three kinds of Christians in the world: believers, nonbelievers, and make-believers. The difference between believers and the other two is repentance.

There is only one that a real man wants to be!

Bee is a miracle of God's doings. Will you be one too?

PRINCIPLES *for* COURAGEOUS MANHOOD

♦ WHAT IS SUBMITTED TO IN LIFE GROWS STRONGER, WHILE WHAT IS RESISTED GROWS WEAKER.

♦ SUBMITTING TO THE LORD GIVES ABILITY TO RESIST THE DEVIL.

♦ REPENTANCE PAVES THE WAY FOR FAITH.

♦ HUMAN SORROW IS ONLY SORROW FOR THE CONSEQUENCES OF SIN. GODLY SORROW IS A SORROW FOR SIN.

♦ THERE ARE THREE KINDS OF CHRISTIANS IN THE WORLD: BELIEVERS, NONBELIEVERS, AND MAKE-BELIEVERS.

♦ THE BIGGEST HYPOCRITE OF ALL IS THE MAN WHO BELIEVES IN HIS HEART IN GOD, BUT WON'T CONFESS IT.

RICK LUND

COURAGE TO CONFRONT YOURSELF

There is a difference between churchianity and Christianity.
In the former, you grow up in church.
In the latter, you grow up in Christ.

Facing his teenage years fatherless, Rick's reality was little different from thousands of American youth. But unlike most, he thought he refused to let it affect him — at least for thirty years.

On a cool Saturday in February when Rick was ten, he noticed the pastor coming up the walkway to their house. Surprised to see him, he and his family hastily tidied up. The pastor took their mother into the family room and the kids huddled nearby in the hallway. Suddenly his older sister, standing closest to the closed door, told her three little brothers that their father was dead. A building inspector, their father had been found dead of a sudden brain aneurysm in his hotel room in a city thirty miles away. Their church family grieved with them and showed them every kindness, but the circumstances dictated that their mother move and start a new life in a new community.

Left without an earthly father, yet not Fatherless, a ray of God's sunshine seemed to follow Rick. Good-looking and athletic, he became the high school quarterback and earned a scholarship to college, where again he earned the top spot as a quarterback. There he fell in love with Ann, a preacher's daughter, the homecoming queen, and the apple of her father's eye. They were married in Iowa, where her father pastored.

After college, Rick attended law school and he and Ann both worked to fulfill their dreams. Sacrificing and struggling, they watched their hard work pay off when Rick finally opened his own law firm. Their economic and social lives began to spiral upwards.

Both having accepted Jesus Christ in their hearts from an early age, they attended church and read their Bibles together. They felt at home at church, socialized outside church, and seemed to fit in everywhere. Rick's quick mind, wit, and ability to make money, put him in good stead with men twice his age, and soon he was accepted in prestigious circles. His practice grew, his income followed, and he and Ann made sure their lifestyle kept up. New homes, great vacations, and eventually two wonderful children born to a world without want, all served to complete their dream of the good life.

As their lifestyle grew, so did the pride and deception of believing in things apart from God. Rick never really had room for Jesus to be the Lord of his life and didn't pray or pursue an intimate relationship with God. Nor did it seem he needed to. Life was good. A few bad business decisions and some deals that went sour still didn't awaken him completely. He resisted those threats by working around them, unwilling to let go of the image that had become so important to him. What he had once cherished most, his marriage to Ann, began to crumble under the weight of the load he'd taken on. Financial complications and social entanglements began to erode the love and trust they'd once known. Unwilling to accept God's help or correction, Rick maintained complete control of his life, which eventually led him into a mountain of unsecured debt.

An opportunity opened for Rick to move his family to a new city, far from the failures that shamed and haunted him. Still unwilling to admit the truth, Rick made excuses for why he and Ann were moving their family to a different community. He said they'd be closer to his mother and brother, which was true. After all, he reasoned, he wasn't a liar. But once he left his familiar surroundings and luxurious lifestyle, God showed Rick a little of what he had become. Deceit was so ingrained in his life and etched in his mind, that he could hardly recognize the truth about himself or others.

On a Thanksgiving holiday after they relocated, he and Ann took their family to her parent's house for dinner. For years Rick and Steve, Ann's brother, had not been able to get along. At their otherwise happy family gathering, Steve and Rick got into a discussion at the family table. It started by talking about their salvation experiences, which they had never discussed before, and ended with an unexpected move of God.

"Rick, God has promises for you of a long, good life," Steve said. Rick was startled to hear one of his deepest fears addressed so openly — the fear that he would die young like his father. "God has security for you and a future that you don't even realize now."

Steve went on with specifics, and suddenly Rick realized that his brother-in-law was truly a changed man, that God was using him to speak to him. Rick started weeping at the table.

They lingered at the table, talking. Rick's heart released cynicism, judgmentalism, and petty jealousies. Thinking that he'd had the ultimate breakthrough, Rick returned to his home and work, believing that God was going to bless him.

Seven months later, Ann asked Rick to accompany her to visit her parents in Florida, where her father was working. The pastor of the church they attended was known for calling people out of the audience to give them a message from God. Hoping for God to bolster his need for importance with some special "word" about rebuilding his hopes and dreams for his future, Rick's motives in going were far from what he received. He stood and sang with the congregation, but knew he was not one of them. As the worship continued, he sensed the tremendous needs of God's people and became aware of those who were humble and truly worshipping God. Finally, his heart was tugged into joining in, and Rick came to a point of total surrender. Rick let go of the hold he had on his own heart as he lifted his hands to the Lord in worship. For the first time since his father died, he let go of the heart he'd guarded — protected by appearances, pride, aloofness, control, and his wit — that kept others from knowing him. Emotion flooded Rick's heart, and he reached out to pray for the people around him. Consumed with a desire for God to meet another's need, Rick forgot about any selfish motives that had led him to the meeting.

As the long service wound to a close and the congregation stood to dismiss, Rick had long since forgotten about any special "word" he was hoping to receive from God. Suddenly the preacher stopped mid-sentence and said, "God has a word for this couple," pointing to Rick and Ann. He said their life had been "messy," but they would "never have to go back to that wilderness again."

After leaving the church that night, a journey began that included forgiveness, healing, and a rebuilding of the love and trust in their marriage. Financially, Rick regained what he'd lost, but his communion with God is now where he finds the true wealth of his life.

Rick was not an unknown quantity when he came to serve with me in the ministry. When my son Paul married Rick's sister, Rick seemed to come with the package. The Cole family watched him grow up, mature, marry, and become successful in business.

When Paul suggested Rick for a committee assignment in the ministry I acquiesced without a question, but in our meetings Rick seemed to let pride in his legal knowledge get in the way of his spiritual life.

When I could tolerate it no longer, I called and asked to meet him privately. In the course of the conversation, he asked why I requested the meeting. My answer did not take long. "I came to ask you to resign your committee appointment."

"What? Why?"

"I can't tell you at this time, but the time will come when you will ask me, and then I'll be able to tell you."

He was frustrated and upset with me, but I could not help the situation.

A few years later I received a call from him when he tracked me down in my hotel room. He told me the nature of his call and said he was coming to a men's meeting I was conducting in a few days. He wanted to see me. When we met before the meeting, he walked up to me, looked me in the eye, took my hand, gripped it, and said, "You were right; I was wrong."

It was my turn to listen intently as he told me the marvelous story of God's transforming work in his life.

"I'm a new man. I have no recollection of the old Rick. My wife tells me how I was, and I don't even recognize it. It's like the old me is a stranger in every way.

"I love reading the Bible. Prayer is something I cannot do without. I love the preaching of the Word. I'm telling you — it's no wonder you dealt with me as you did. I must have been a pain in your backside. It's so good to walk with the Lord."

The difference in him is the difference between "churchianity" and Christianity. In the former you grow up in church; in the latter you grow up in Christ. Some men put on religious trappings becoming, as Christ called the Pharisees, "whitewashed tombs," dead inside but with a real good appearance. Man whitewashes; God washes white.

The "church wise" are as deceived as the "street wise," playing the game, going through the motions of their religion. Rick was so good at it, he even played the game with himself. Ensnared by his own pride and self-importance, Rick could have lived blind forever. But he had the courage to confront himself and see himself in the glaring light of God's love and truth.

During the course of the meeting, I had him stand and tell the men what had happened. They stood and cheered him when he finished. To God be the glory!

It took courage for Rick to humble himself before God and others, but he did it.

When Rick came and confessed to me openly and honestly, I put my trust in him again. I love being with Rick now. He is an excellent prayer partner, and his testimony becomes more spiritually potent day by day.

P R I N C I P L E S *for* COURAGEOUS MANHOOD

♦ THERE'S A DIFFERENCE BETWEEN "CHURCHIANITY" AND CHRISTIANITY. IN THE FORMER YOU GROW UP IN CHURCH; IN THE LATTER YOU GROW UP IN CHRIST.

♦ MAN WHITEWASHES; GOD WASHES WHITE.

ELEVEN

JOHN BINKLEY

COURAGE TO
DO THE LITTLE THING

*If you want to know God's plan for your life,
just do the next little thing He tells you to do.*

John looked at the audience and noted the men of influence that Roger, the event organizer, had pointed out earlier. The ambassador from Panama, the Supreme Court justice, the secretaries on the President's Cabinet, the influential lawyers and professionals. Then he cleared his throat and started in.

"All work is ministry, whether it's your business, your hospital, or your government — it is all ministry," he stated with his Texas accent. "And all ministry is done as unto the Lord. When you work for God, you don't compromise your values, your work ethic, or your integrity. You cannot be bought. You pursue excellence personally and stop comparing yourself to others. Don't worry about God's total plan for your life, just do what you're supposed to do and do it with all your heart. Then God will make a way for you."

After quoting from the Bible and ministering for about another twenty minutes through an interpreter, John led the crowd to close their eyes and repeat a prayer after them to receive Jesus Christ into their hearts.

Roger cried after the meeting. After many years of plowing the fields in the hearts of his native Nicaraguans, he was beginning to see huge harvests. Other ministers reached the masses of the Nicaraguan population, but men like John came to minister to the leadership. Roger's influence brought them, John's message impressed them, and God saved them by the hundreds. Nicaragua was changing.

As Roger pointed out to John the people who had received Christ, including a Supreme Court justice, John shook his head in amazement. How did he get here? He thought back to a verse he'd memorized ten years earlier: *Seest thou a man diligent in his business? he shall stand before kings; he shall not stand before mean* [obscure] *men* (Proverbs 22:29).

Back in 1980, John made a habit of giving his basic tithes and offerings to the church. Then one night in 1986, as he read the Williams paraphrase of the New Testament, a verse from Mark 7:6-13 leaped off the page at him. It said that he could not give his gifts to God without taking care of his parents.

Years before, John had learned the principle, "If you want to know God's plan for your life, just do the next little thing He tells you to do." So it was natural for him to do what he believed God wanted him to do, and he and his wife, Sharon, started supporting their parents with a little each month.

John had also applied this principle when he left the insurance business to work in sales for a man who was just starting out. John well remembers the early years when he would leave the office and rack up $1000 in expenses before he made his first sale. He would pray Psalm 112, the whole chapter, inserting his name wherever it said "a man," or "the man." He prayed, believing in the truth of Proverbs 22:29, that diligence and perseverance would set him apart from other men. John was convinced God had a plan for him, so he went boldly, overcoming obstacles as they appeared. John made the second, third, fourth, fifth, sixth, and seventh sales ever made at the owner's new business. Within two years, he became the vice-president, and in three years the part-owner.

When he became part-owner, it was in partnership with two other people. It wasn't long before a financial slide spelled disaster for them all. John was "unequally yoked" with his partners and couldn't exercise decisive authority. Fortunately, they had a buyout clause in their partnership for the enterprise. It took courage, but John made them an offer, and they accepted. The year after he took the little step of helping his parents, he became the sole possessor of one company and two million dollars of debt.

Advisors to John didn't think much of his taking over the company by himself. But John's confidence wasn't in the company, nor his employees, nor even his own abilities and skills. His confidence was in the God of his salvation. If God could turn his life around, could make his partners willing to sell in order to free him from his "unequal yoke," then God was certainly able to turn a business around.

John was right. His counselors were wrong. He paid off a seven-and-a-half year note three years early. Within a few years, the business was skyrocketing into the seven-figures and surging upwards. John continued doing the next little thing he knew God wanted him to do, and it seemed to push the business even higher. He started investing his time, not just his money, in getting away from his business to go on short missions trips.

John's first trip to Nicaragua was in 1995, as part of a ministry team. That year, his company broke all previous records. The next year, he went back alone to preach for Roger, and saw many of the business professionals of several cities won to Christ. His interpreter said it was the best layman's message he'd ever heard preached — and all John did was share the principles that had worked for him.

In 1996, John left the country five times for international missions trips, and his business increased over the record-breaking year before by 16 percent. The next year, 1997, John again left the country five times, but instead of suffering or slowing down, his business increased a dramatic 42 percent.

John has now traveled to twenty-eight nations, mostly for ministry purposes, and has never seen his business suffer a day. He believes that by "doing the next little thing" God tells him to do, he has received God's blessing on his business and his life. As a result of John honoring God in obedience to the "little things," God has honored John.

John says he felt like a fool for not supporting his and his wife's parents when he first realized what the Bible said. Too often, men feel like fools only after they've parted with their money, not because they didn't part with it soon enough.

Consider how seriously God regards the disobedience to His command. Once understood, it is to be obeyed.

John recently spoke to a group of men in Australia about honoring their parents, and he had a dramatic response. One of the men went home and told his wife what he had heard. She immediately called her parents and learned they had been sick and couldn't pay the doctor. It was a joy for that couple to send her parents a check. The phone call was a "little thing," like John's, but the rewards were great.

John was probably more pleased than they were when he heard the report. He was thrilled and blessed that someone had listened and acted on one "little thing" from God's Word. God only shows you the next thing to do in your life, not where you'll be ten years from now. He develops you into what He wants you to be, and what He wants you to do, which is often beyond your own wildest imagination.

Nothing is born in maturity. Everything is grown into it.

Knowing the will of God for your life is just doing in obedience the next thing God leads you to do. Do the next thing God tells you to do, and you will always be in the will of God.

PRINCIPLES *for* COURAGEOUS MANHOOD

♦ ALL WORK IS MINISTRY, WHETHER IT'S YOUR BUSINESS, YOUR HOSPITAL, OR YOUR GOVERNMENT — IT IS ALL MINISTRY.

♦ IF YOU WANT TO KNOW GOD'S PLAN FOR YOUR LIFE, JUST DO THE NEXT LITTLE THING HE TELLS YOU TO DO.

TWELVE

TOM DEUSCHLE

COURAGE TO OVERCOME THE NEGATIVE

Don't let someone else create your world,
for when they do, they will always create it too small.

No support from the States. No missions board. No money. No way of earning. No good reason to stay. No desire to leave. No church home. No old friends. And not going anywhere except forward. That was Tom Deuschle in 1980, one year after buying a ticket to Africa and finding himself in the middle of a civil war, alone and broke. No chance of building one of the largest multicultural churches in central Africa. No chance of rescuing thousands of refugees, bringing medical and food relief. No chance of influencing the destiny of a nation that was not even his by birth.

At age eighteen, Tom made a list of what he wanted to accomplish in life. He wanted to preach. He wanted to fly airplanes. He wanted to go to Africa. He wanted to get married. There were other things that he determined to do.

Tom felt like it was God Who was telling him to go to Rhodesia. When he first felt the call, he didn't even know it was in Africa. He attended two years of Bible college, then returned home to work in sales with his father for two years. His dad, a successful salesman, was the first to teach Tom how to succeed in life.

"You see those guys going to Donut Hut?" he asked Tom, motioning to a group of salesmen heading out the door of the office where they worked. "They're going to drink coffee and complain about how hard it is to make a sale. They're going to talk about how tough life is, why they can't get ahead, and by the time they start selling today, they're going to have talked themselves out of selling anything.

"Tom," his dad turned to looked at him squarely, "I don't ever want to see you going to Donut Hut."

Tom was young, but could see a little of what made his dad successful — and it wasn't a fear of doughnuts. Tom realized that to create a competitive edge, he'd have to be focused and positive and stay around people who were the same. He also realized he didn't want to sell for the rest of his life, as the call to Africa grew stronger.

From his short career in sales, Tom saved enough money to go to Rhodesia, in the heart of central Africa. Leaving or selling most of his belongings, Tom packed up some clothes and left the security of his home in Colorado to arrive in a country deeply torn by civil war.

The British had left the former colony several years earlier, leaving a group of white settlers who created a government and developed the economy. Black nationals resented being barred from government and from most of the economic benefits in their homeland, so groups of freedom fighters developed to oust the white ruling party. The white farmers who had given up everything in England to develop the land they'd purchased were equally unwilling to budge, and soon a civil war was raging in the bushlands, where men who grew up together killed each other, and no one was winning.

When Tom arrived, he looked for every opportunity to minister in any way. He started teaching a Catholic youth group, then he taught at an African Bible college. Other schools wanted him as well, and there was always witnessing to be done on the streets and in people's homes.

Tom found most everyone in his new war-weary home accepted his message of comfort and help — young or old, black or white, rich or poor. Once he ministered to their needs, they received his gospel message. They were looking to him with piercing questions, and he gave them real answers.

Tom would travel to the outlying farming areas and listen to the "agri-alert" radio system that networked the farmers and helped protect them from skirmishes in their areas. He would hear the report and head straight for the battleground. There, he would often arrive at the same time as the military and emergency teams. Besides the physical injuries, the atrocities on both sides cut deep wounds in people's hearts, and Tom battled hatred and bitterness on both sides as he ministered the love of Jesus Christ.

Tom's money lasted three months, then he had to count on offerings of money, food, or gas from the local people. That's when he started hearing the negative remarks — it can't be done; you need a missions board to sponsor you. He was a strange sight — a missionary to Africa asking the Africans for support. Tom tried to steer clear of those who would drain his ministry of energy, just as he had avoided the salesmen in the donut shop. When he did run into them, he loved them, but he simply didn't listen to them.

Within Tom's second year in Africa, the warring parties agreed to a new form of government for a new nation they would call Zimbabwe. They called a free election, and the head of one of the freedom fighters' groups took the reins of government. The strong economy continued to grow, making Zimbabwe one of the most stable economies in all of Africa at that time.

In the aftermath of the war, Tom found himself an outsider. The nation was embroiled in a war of words, and the rhetoric of racism rang everywhere. As an American, Tom felt their prejudice. Blacks were angry when they discovered Tom was ministering to whites. Whites were angry when they found he was ministering to blacks. People told him he'd have to choose one group or another. Soon Tom didn't fit in anywhere, but as he continued to minister everywhere, people continued to support him, and his ministry and reputation grew.

On a trip to the U.S. during his third year in Africa, Tom fell in love with Bonnie, whom he had met in Bible college. She had been one of the Oral Roberts University World Action Singers, a former beauty queen from Kansas, and Tom knew he'd have to stand in line behind all the other young men looking to win Bonnie's heart — none of whom lived on pennies in Africa. But Tom was accustomed to overcoming the negative. On this visit, when their paths crossed, Tom won her heart. When Bonnie realized Tom was the one for her, which meant Africa would be her home, she boldly said good-bye to the world she knew and accepted his one-way ticket to Africa as her wedding gift.

The next year, Tom and Bonnie felt strongly that they were to start a multicultural church with a strong Word-based message and an outreach to the community. Tom preached and Bonnie sang, friends and converts pitched in to help, and within two years of opening the church doors, theirs was the largest multicultural church in the capitol city of Harare. Today their church is one of the largest in all of Africa. Their congregation has influence in the highest ranks of government, and Tom's message of Christ's healing power is helping to shape the destiny of his adopted nation.

The courage Tom showed in overcoming the negative to follow a vague dream toward his mission in life has resulted in miracles in the lives of those he serves. When nearby Mozambique needed relief due to their civil war, Tom's people rallied to the cause. After going to the U.S. to try to raise relief support, Tom returned to Zimbabwe armed with food and clothing. His team drove trucks to the relief villages that sprang up on the border between their nations and disbursed necessities to the refugees who had fled the fighting for their lives, with no earthly possessions.

On one such occasion, the team had given out all the adult clothing, leaving a long line of ragged children that stretched down the road as far as he could see. Soon, only one bag of clothing was left. Praying over that bag as they doled out the precious items, the relief workers continued to clothe each child in turn. The children kept coming until the end of the line was within sight, but the workers knew the bag could not possibly have enough clothes for all they'd dressed already, as well as all those still waiting. They continued to pray, and to their astonishment, the last garment was not used until the last child was clothed. Today the empty bag sits in a special place in Tom's church as their own war trophy — the war waged for the relief of mankind in order to win the hearts of men to Christ.

Miracles of God's saving grace through Tom and Bonnie's work can be seen in every outreach, on every front, in every service, and the financial miracles keep coming as well. Today, using only African money, Tom is building a $30 million church, with outreach facilities attached. He allows foreigners to support the relief efforts and special outreaches, but the church itself is built only with African money. Tom believes the people of Africa need the opportunity to support their own church and have their own success, like any other part of the world. Just as they supported the ministry from the day he ran out of money, they have supported the church they helped to build.

Today, Tom has gone from no known source of support other than the God Who sent him, to no known source of support other than the God Who sent him. That hasn't changed, but Tom is rich spiritually, and his congregation members are the happy recipients of his heavenly wealth.

Buying a ticket to a country where you have never been, where you know no one, and know nothing about them, is not exactly my idea of preparing to succeed. Besides, Tom didn't even know exactly what he was going to do. But Tom wouldn't let others create his world for him. He knew the only way to succeed was to be willing to fail, and he was prepared for success by not fearing failure. Arriving in Rhodesia when the war was on, Tom wondered why God had sent him to such a place. Terror and tension gripped everyone — friends and enemies mingled freely on the street in the daytime, but killed each other under cover of night. Only now that he has one of the largest Christian outreaches on the continent does he understand it.

When God promised Israel he would defeat their enemies so they could possess the land, He described His strategy for victory: *Little by little I will drive them out from before you, until you have increased, and you inherit the land* (Exodus 23:30 NKJV). The pattern never varies. It's God's method to occupy the place He wants you to be.

When he first landed in Rhodesia, Tom had neither the anointing nor the faith for the miracle he experienced in clothing the refugees years later. He read in the Bible of the miracle of the loaves and fishes (see Matthew 14:17-21), but never knew he would see such a miracle himself. A plastic bag with a few clothes in it is the evidence of his maturity in faith and in favor with God.

Moses told Israel to build a pile of stones as a memorial to their supernatural deliverance from Egypt. A plastic bag is Tom's "pile of stones" as a testimony to the miraculous power of God.

Arriving in Africa, Tom could barely accept responsibility for his own actions, much less that of a nation. How did he grow to such a full measure of responsibility? By his willingness to serve. Jesus Himself taught us the principle, *Yet it shall not be so among you; but whoever desires to become great among you, let him be your servant* (Matthew 20:26 NKJV). The more you serve, the greater you become. Too many men want to be served rather than serve, and they remain mediocre throughout life. Tom served, and his ministry became great.

The way to excellence is being led by the Spirit of God.

A kid with courage added to his faith has become a man among men. Tom did not allow others to create his world for him. When they were negative, he was positive. The proverb says, *Stop listening to teaching that contradicts what you know is right* (Proverbs 19:27 TLB).

What's your story?

P R I N C I P L E S *for* COURAGEOUS MANHOOD

♦ DON'T LET OTHERS CREATE YOUR WORLD, FOR WHEN THEY DO, THEY WILL ALWAYS MAKE IT TOO SMALL.

♦ THE ONLY WAY TO SUCCEED IS TO BE WILLING TO FAIL.

♦ THE MORE YOU SERVE, THE GREATER YOU BECOME.

THIRTEEN

DAVID FOWLER

COURAGE TO FATHER

Prayer produces intimacy.

The boy ran from toy to toy, screaming as he picked things up, crying when his mother told him to put them down, fighting her every demand by stepping just one foot too far beyond the boundaries she set. The crowded room became chaotic as the child threw fits every few minutes and refused to play calmly.

"Let me take him," David offered the screaming child's mother.

"Oh, no, don't bother," she said sheepishly, "he's just in those terrible twos."

"I can help if you want me to," David said, his broad smile and inviting attitude welcome, even to a nerve-rattled toddler's mother.

"Well, if he's bothering you...."

David picked up the boy and took him into another room. With five of his own, he had developed some fathering techniques that children found soothing. He and his wife Toni host hundreds of people in their home each year, and home-school their own small children. David knew he could help both the child and parent with a lesson in love and security.

Taking the child to a quiet room adjacent to the family room where their guests were visiting, David held the boy stationary within his arms, speaking soothingly to him, and telling him the wonderful things God had planned for his life. Immobilizing the child brought hostile rebellion at first, then calm stillness, as the child surrendered to the physical boundaries of David's embrace and listened to his reassuring voice. The child's emotion soon changed from somber to happy, as the security that someone in his life was in control took effect. Minutes later, David emerged with his new friend following him, bright-faced, happy, eager to play, and no longer petulant or angry. David was familiar with the stunned look on the mother's face, as he has helped many a parent see a change in their toddler.

David knows what works with his children. He rattles off their names, ages, and special interests without hesitating. If textbook studies can be believed, when David's children hit the workforce starting in about 2004, they should become one of the great American families of leaders, artists, government servants, and professionals, completely fulfilled in God's purpose for each of their lives.

Only a few of David's parenting skills were learned at home. He conscientiously developed as a father by taking the good, subtracting the bad, adding biblical principles, multiplying love, and dividing his attention fairly between his many children. He has declared a mission in life to acknowledge and respect his children as people and to help nurture their purpose in life. When he instructs or corrects his children, he tells them what their names mean and why they have those names. Joshua David, Naloni Lee, Samuel Paul,

Daniel Michael, and Christopher Caleb — each child knows the meanings for both first and middle names.

Joshua was three years old when David first went to his room one night, sat down, and began singing songs of praise to God and praying earnestly with Joshua. Joshua looked wide-eyed at his father, as if he were wishing to get back to "Twinkle, Twinkle, Little Star." But David knew he was establishing a pattern, one that he has not varied in Joshua's eleven years.

David and Toni lead busy lives, but at night, when the dinner dishes are cleared, David leads his little congregation in worship by sitting on the floor in one of their bedrooms singing, then each taking a turn to pray, followed by reciting the Lord's Prayer together in unison. The evening draws to a close as David scratches their backs and talks about ponies, swimming lessons, homeschool, and anything else that comes to their minds. David knows that prayer produces intimacy. He came by that knowledge in a difficult way.

David is bent on success as a father in the same way he was bent on succeeding in work, which started at a very young age. By age nine, David's dad had his sons working in a profit-sharing business with him, remodeling lake homes in their resort community. The three boys worked hard, along with two paid workers, and the profits rolled in. His dad taught them money management, responsibility, and the benefits of having a good attitude. At the same time, David acted five nights a week for five years in the nationally renowned "Passion Play" near his home.

At age fourteen, David branched out of the family business and went to work as a dishwasher in a swank resort hotel. Within a few months, one of the cooks left, and the manager offered David the job. Under the manager's tutelage, David's career as a cook led to night shift supervisor. Then he was hired away by a restaurant that wanted him to help design their kitchen, menu, and become assistant manager. When the manager was forced to resign for health reasons, David became the restaurant manager — all before he turned sixteen.

Deeply interested in history and civil government in school, David excelled in his studies, as well as sports. He was elected class president for two years, then student body president for one. David was fascinated by the government that was formed from biblical principles, and his studies confirmed his heartfelt commitment to God. He pursued a nomination to attend Boys' State, a political invitation-only camp for boys going into their senior year of high school. There he met Bill Clinton, Jim Guy Tucker, and other politicians, that resulted in invitations to Washington, D.C., years later when Bill Clinton became President. David's dad was proud of his son's accomplishments, though he preferred to show it by supporting David's sports activities. He was at the finish line when David placed first in a marathon against hundreds of runners, and he never missed a home basketball game.

At age sixteen, David moved from his parent's home to the hotel where he had returned to work, and by age nineteen, he was the general manager of the same resort hotel where he'd washed dishes just five years earlier. When he was twenty, he moved to a major U.S. city where an international hotel chain hired him as manager of catering sales for their four-star hotel, the youngest in the history of their company.

"I just had to meet you for myself," the president of the hotel chain told David as he shook his hand weeks after David started work. "I came here purposely just to meet you, because I couldn't believe they were giving someone your age this responsibility!"

While working there, David learned the audio and video business from the in-house firm that rented equipment to hotel customers. Seeing David's talent and work ethic, the owner of the firm, the nation's largest provider of rental equipment to the hotel and convention industry, hired him away and started him on a career in audio and video systems. David found his new skills in high demand in the Christian realm, and eventually traveled with many Christian music artists as a sound technician. By age twenty-two, he managed all of his firm's audio and video rental offices in his city.

David's dad took great pride in David's career successes, bringing friends and business associates to "his son's" hotel to brag about his accomplishments. But to David, his father talked only of himself and his own businesses and ministries. David never had an opportunity to bounce career ideas off his Dad or get encouragement for his own calling. In his early twenties, with a string of successes behind him, David felt bankrupt, personally defeated — and he didn't know why. He had everything — great career opportunities, wonderful friends, financial success, and even a good relationship with God. But something was missing.

About that time, David heard a man speak for a few minutes at a church conference, and he insisted his brother attend with him that night when the man was preaching. David and his brother held hands at the end of the meeting and prayed together. It mended their own relationship and started a close friendship and true brotherhood between them. David found out the minister was heading for Houston, the hometown of a beautiful woman he'd just met. Toni encouraged David to come to Houston and stay with her family.

"Prayer produces intimacy," the minister said in one of the sessions. "Fathers have to learn to pray for their children to become intimate with them. You must first talk to God about your children, then talk to your children about God. It's the prophetic role."

David bowed his head as hot tears sprang up and began to run down his face. Memories flashed through his mind of all the churches he'd sat in with his father, all the people he'd seen his father pray with, and not one memory held an image of his dad praying with him. He remembered his dad talking about his own ministry, especially during a time when he pastored, but David couldn't remember his dad ever talking to him about David's ministry, or what God might have planned for David's life. He realized what was missing in his life — intimacy. He'd known his dad only superficially, and the emptiness of the relationship had finally hit him.

Tears rolled down his face as the grief for what he'd never known welled up inside him. Throughout the entire meeting David sat weeping sadly, yet grateful for the feelings that were being loosed within him. The minister spoke kindly to David and offered a "father's hug," praying for and with him. David again wept as the affirmation flowed through him like a warm medicine, healing what he never knew was injured, binding together what he never knew was unraveled. For the first time, David believed God might actually fulfill what was in his heart as a young man — according to the prophet Jeremiah's words, God had a plan for him that was good, not evil, to give him hope and a future. (See Jeremiah 29:11.) David went on to marry Toni. They co-founded a thriving teen missions organization, work closely with several ministries, and unofficially disciple many people in their home.

Today, David won't allow anything to stand in the way of his prayer times with his children, nor to ruin the call of God on their lives. He is intent on nurturing them as individuals, paying attention to the whole person, not simply the athletics or scholastics.

Whether providing the boundaries for his two-year-old or gently leading his eleven-year-old into "putting away childish things," David is completely fulfilled in his role as a father. Realizing the awesome task of developing his boys into men of God and his daughter into a woman of God, he has grown ever more dependent on God to fulfill His desires for himself and his family. He knows prayer is the glue that creates the bond between him and his wife as well as him and his kids. And as he's grown more mature, his prayers for his dad are producing an intimacy in the relationship that they have never known before.

There have been times when I thought nothing would surprise, shock, or amaze me anymore. I thought I was foolproof. But David did all three to me. The enterprising businessman, devoted husband, and faithful father he is now is something wonderful to see.

In our first meeting, he interrupted me with his crying. Since he was sitting on the front row, I felt I had to stop ministering and ask him, "What's the matter?"

"You're teaching us that prayer produces intimacy," he stammered with tears still rolling down his face. "My dad was a pastor until I was in the third grade, and I'm twenty-three now. Though he's prayed with others, he has never prayed with me one time."

That revelation has furnished the catalyst for the father he is today. His children will never be without a father's love, care, and prayer. David has been encouraged by what God said about Abraham, and he wants it said about him. *For I know him, that he will command his children and his household after him* (Genesis 18:19.).

Abraham was a man who obtained righteousness by faith. He tithed, rescued his nephew Lot after he was carried away captive, and "commanded his family after him." David is chalking up three out of four, and working on rescuing others who have been carried away captive by sin and Satan.

Abraham's responsibilities to his son were fourfold: circumcise his son, find him a wife, teach him a trade, and give him an inheritance. It is the same for those who are descendants of faithful Abraham, who believe in Christ and have obtained righteousness by faith.

Circumcise his son. Circumcising your child in the New Testament represents a cutting away of that which is unclean, meaning an assurance your child knows Christ as Savior.

Find him a wife. In the world today, it is not uncommon in many places for parents to find their sons the wife they are to marry. In America, it represents to us teaching a son or daughter how to be a good husband or wife. In the days of Abraham they did not marry the one they loved, but loved the one they married. These days men marry the one they love, then don't love the one they marry. We have to change it back.

It is imperative for a father to teach his child that God has given him a gift. God has given the child one thing to give one time to one person in one lifetime. It is so intrinsically valuable, so precious, so significant to the covenant of marriage, God has given just one gift. It's the gift of virginity. It is up to the father to pass to the child the reverence for the gift of God within him.

Teach him a trade. In days gone by, sons followed their fathers in a trade. In America, we see that they go to school or gain an apprenticeship to learn one. But sons still follow their fathers in ministry. If God did not want sons to inherit ministries, He would not be known as the God of Abraham, Isaac and Jacob. Giving a son a good work ethic will provide him with the basic necessity of any trade he chooses.

Give him an inheritance. Giving him an inheritance is leaving a vital legacy. Lands and monies are a great inheritance, but a legacy of faith is greater than all. John wrote, *I have no greater joy than to hear that my children walk in truth* (3 John 1:4).

David Fowler has thrown himself into the task of providing his sons and daughters the same love and security Abraham provided for his. God's commendation is all David wants to hear.

So dedicated is David that nothing will shatter his children's understanding of a godly life, that he would even confront his own father about his grandchildren. So convicted is David that prayer produces intimacy, he now prays with and for his own father.

David's courageous manhood has given his children a better way.

❈

P R I N C I P L E S *for* COURAGEOUS MANHOOD

* PRAYER PRODUCES INTIMACY.

* YOU MUST FIRST TALK TO GOD ABOUT YOUR CHILDREN BEFORE YOU TALK TO YOUR CHILDREN ABOUT GOD.

* IF GOD DID NOT WANT SONS TO INHERIT MINISTRIES, HE WOULD NOT BE KNOWN AS THE GOD OF ABRAHAM, ISAAC, AND JACOB.

FOURTEEN

SULIASI KURULO

COURAGE
IN FAITH

Faith puts no limits on God; God puts no limits on faith.

The man walked to the front of the auditorium carrying his stick — the magic stick with the secret powers that he used on people for good, and for evil. Total silence enveloped the crowded auditorium, where 15,000 Papua New Guineans were gathered. The witch doctor was challenging the preacher! Suliasi Kurulo stopped in the middle of his sermon and listened as the man bellowed.

"You can't fight our gods," the witch doctor yelled, raising his stick and shaking it at Suli. "If you think your God is more powerful than ours, you're going to have to prove it!" Suli was startled, as was the rest of the crowd, but he had no fear of the outcome.

It was ten years earlier that Suli had left home with only six pennies in his pocket to witness to people about Jesus Christ. He never imagined it was the start of one of the world's largest church movements, or that he'd end up in far-flung lands like Papua New Guinea or Zaire.

His wife Mere had stayed home, tending the garden and their child, praying for the best. Things had been more comfortable when Suli worked full-time as a civil engineer, but he was intent now to work full-time for God, and Mere comforted herself in knowing that God was all-powerful and would see them through.

Within months of leaving the house by foot on that first day, Suli had won dozens of people to Christ, and God had provided for all of Suli and Mere's needs. Teenagers who had been won to Christ started following Suli home, begging to join him in reaching others with the Gospel. With no means of feeding or housing these young people, Suli and Mere sought the Lord for a decision. They soon attached a tent to the back of their rented house and had seventy young people staying with them — teenagers who vowed not to date or leave them until every home in Fiji had been reached with the gospel message. The boldness that God had put in Suli to share Christ was now being birthed in the hearts of these young men and women.

Suli sized up the witch doctor who was now taunting him and saw him as a nuisance. He was about to make an important point and really wanted to get on with his message. He knew there was no power greater than the power of God, but did the people?

There was the time when he and Mere had prayed over a mob of men who had threatened to come after them and stop a crusade they were holding. As they prayed, Mere saw a vision of angels coming down from heaven and encompassing the tent where they held their meetings. Without thinking more about it, they held the meetings, which proved to be enormously successful and without incident.

A year later they learned what had happened when one of the men who was in on the raid that night became a devout Christian and told the story. He came with van loads of men in a rage, intent on destroying the meetings and killing or harming Suli. But when they were within earshot of the tent, they all became numb and were unable to drive away or open the doors to the vans. All through the gospel message they sat in their vans listening, until finally the numbness wore off and the drivers were able to drive away.

Another mighty miracle occurred when his young protégés had completely evangelized Fiji and decided to go to the Solomon Islands. The young evangelists trained the Solomon Islanders and set out door-to-door just as they had in Fiji. But when they came to the edge of Kwaio territory, which was the next region on their maps, the Solomon Islanders pulled back.

"We can't go in there!" they said.

"But we must!" the Fijians insisted. "We've been sent on a mission to reach every home in the Solomon Islands!"

The Fijians couldn't be talked out of it, even though the Solomon Islanders explained that their own relatives had died in Kwaio territory, that the Kwaio were ruthless killers and cannibals, and that every missionary who'd approached their territory for a hundred years had been murdered. When the Fijians stood firm in their determination to go, the hearts of the Solomon Islanders were touched.

"How can we let them risk their lives to reach our brothers in Kwaio when we're not even willing to risk our own?" they reasoned. "We'll go with you! If you die, we all die."

For a week the young men fasted and prayed, until they knew that it was time to go. When they entered the area, many Kwaio became Christians, but as they moved into the interior, the village leaders kept them at spear-point. The young evangelists demanded to talk to Haribo, the high chief of one village. When an audience was finally granted, the old chief met them at the door of his hut and swept his hand for them to enter.

"I'm glad you're here," he said warmly. "None of my gods are answering me, so perhaps yours will."

They ministered the gospel message to Haribo, and he answered them. "I'm 120 years old, and I've worshipped the god of the sun, and the god of the moon, but now God has brought you here to show me the one true God."

As they encouraged him, only fifteen minutes after he received Christ, he closed his eyes and died. The Kwaio villagers were furious.

"Your God killed our chief!" they cried.

The young men tried to minister the Gospel to them, to tell them Haribo was now in heaven. Two agonizing hours went by as their predicament became more and more deadly. Then suddenly, as the young men were praying, Haribo came back to life. He told the chieftains to gather the people. The Kwaio were so fierce, they lived far apart to keep from killing each other, so only seventy people could be found in a short amount of time. When they gathered, Haribo told them his story.

"When I went to sleep," he said, "two men with wings took me to a city where there was beautiful music. I met a man named Abraham, and another named Elijah."

At this, the young evangelists gasped, since they had never mentioned these names, nor did Haribo have any way of ever hearing those names before.

"I saw the beautiful city with streets of gold and heard the most beautiful music," Haribo continued. "And the men told me, that's the city where people go when they die if they believe Jesus. Then they took me to another city, where there was agony and death, and they told me that's where people go if they don't believe Jesus."

He turned the meeting over to the young men and they concluded with, "How many people want to know Jesus?" Seventy hands shot into the air.

Within six years, thirty-two Christian villages were built around churches and 4000 Kwaio were saved. For the Kwaio, their ancestral and native gods are so entrenched in their home life that repentance means burning their old houses and belongings and moving to the Christian village to follow Christ.

Suli also thought of the pygmies, an unreached people in Zaire, where God gave even greater success. In 1992, evangelists whom Suli had sent arrived in the pygmy territory, where the people lived in trees and thought of themselves and lived as animals. The strategy to reach the pygmies was "tree-to-tree" instead of "door-to-door" and involved an entire mind and spirit transformation. The missionaries helped them with medicine and hygiene, and they slowly won converts, totaling 5,000 by 1994. The work multiplied, and by 1998, 200,000 pygmies were converted and living in Christian villages.

Suli now stood in front of the stadium filled with people, with all these great successes behind him, being challenged by a witch doctor who was greatly admired, feared, and respected by all in attendance. He knew from the pygmy experience how easy it is for men to see themselves as "grasshoppers," as Israel once did when they were too fearful to enter Canaan. (See Numbers 13 and 14.) But the Spirit that once arose in David when the giant challenged the Israelite army (see 1 Samuel 17) moved within Suli. He knew the Bible said he was more than a conqueror through Jesus Christ (see Romans 8:37), and everything within him rose to the challenge of the witch doctor who dared defy his God.

"Yahhhhh," the witch doctor yelled. He threw his magic rod at Suli like a javelin, but Suli caught the stick in the air and broke it over his knee. When the stick broke, the people gasped in amazement and horror. In the next moment, they broke out in rejoicing and praise to God for the black magic to be broken and defeated. Suli turned to the witch doctor and said, "In the name of Jesus I rebuke you!"

The man fell to his knees under the power of God. He struggled to get up, but couldn't. The crowd, now singing with wild enthusiasm, spontaneously rose from their seats to dance. Suli pointed toward the man as he wobbled about on his hands and knees. "You cannot stand until you confess that Jesus Christ is Lord," Suli commanded.

"Jesus is Lord," the witch doctor said, hanging his head. Knowing he was defeated, and sincerely desiring the power of the true God, the man repeated it again, then stood up — a new creation in Christ!

Miracles continue to follow Suli as his ministry flourishes throughout Fiji, the South Pacific, and as far as Africa — anywhere there is an unreached people in the world. With such faith, the ministry will continue to expand, as Suli is raising up the next generation to follow him. Sixty of the original seventy young people are now working in full-time ministry, pastoring, working as missionaries, and telling everyone they know of the wonderful God Who so providentially protects and keeps them throughout their adventure in evangelism.

❈

When Suliasi left home with just six pennies in his pocket, he was completely dependent on God for everything in life. All he could do was trust God for what he needed.

On that first day, he went to the bus stop to begin his ministry, knocking on doors in the daytime and preaching at night. Standing in front of the open door of the bus, he did not know what to do. It would leave in five minutes, and he had no money for the fare. "I've got to start somewhere and this is it," he thought.

Stepping toward the bus, not knowing what the driver would say when he entered, a woman's voice called out to him. He turned to see who it was.

"Brother Suli, where are you going?" the lady asked as she approached him.

"Going to preach," he replied.

"Do you have any money?" she inquired.

"No."

"Wait a minute," she commanded, getting closer to where he was.

"Here." Holding out her hand as he began to step on the bus, she handed him a ten dollar bill. That ten dollar gift was the beginning of a soulwinning crusade that has spread across the world.

The foundation is the most important part of any building. The taller the structure, the deeper the foundation must be. It is no different with God's ministries. *Without faith it is impossible to please him* (Hebrews 11:6). Faith is the substance upon which God's work on earth is built. Faith is the foundation upon which the superstructure rests. For a great ministry, God begins with the minister having nothing else to depend on but faith in Him. Faith puts no limits on God; God puts no limits on faith.

Everything in life is done in increments. Live one day at a time, eat one bite at a time, say one word at a time, witness to one person at a time, until the whole is done. Pastor Suliasi grew in faith one miracle at a time over the years. To him, the miracles he sees now, in their immensity, seem like getting the first ten dollar bill. Faith has not changed; it is still faith. But it has matured, growing stronger and larger. Now he ministers not to just the ones, but to the thousands and hundreds of thousands.

In recent days Suli needed a place other than a rented group of stores in which to house the ministry. He prayed, planned, and prepared for a new three-story complex that, when finished, would cost $750,000. When he received the bill for the architect's drawings, he knew the design was worth every penny of the $22,000 charged, but he didn't have the money. Within a few days, the firm discounted the charges to only $12,000. That Friday, Suli went home and prayed with Mere, trusting God for the money on Monday. No money came on Monday, but the president of the architectural firm called Suli and said, "I believe we should just give you these plans at no cost." Suli broke ground for the building with only $38,000 in the bank, and paid for it as it was built. There were times when they threatened to stop building for lack of funds, but the money was always there at the precise moment it was needed.

"I never worried," he acknowledges. "I had faith."

Faith is like the wind. You can't see it. You can only see its results. The swaying of a tree, banners fluttering, and hair blowing are some simple results of the wind's presence. So faith, like the wind, is known by its products or results. To say you have faith, but you have nothing to show for it, is not faith. It may be belief, but even the devils believe in God. Yet they don't have faith. Faith is not admitting there is a God, but trusting Him with your total life.

Whether it is greater to have faith in God to heal the sick, build a building without anything to build it with, or see pygmies and cannibals saved, who can tell? It is all great faith.

That great teacher of the Word, LaFayette Scales, says, "There is little faith, faith, and great faith. All believers have some measure of faith. For the nation of Israel, their faith was evident in their results — Egypt was the land of not enough, the wilderness was the place of just enough, but Canaan was the land of more than enough. That's faith, little faith, and great faith in action."

Courageous manhood means acting in great faith.

Pastor Suliasi had the courage to act on his belief in God and became a man of faith. He is a modern-day hero in contemporary Christianity.

❖

P R I N C I P L E S *for* COURAGEOUS MANHOOD

- ♦ FAITH PUTS NO LIMITS ON GOD; GOD PUTS NO LIMITS ON FAITH.

- ♦ FAITH IS LIKE THE WIND. YOU CAN'T SEE IT. YOU CAN ONLY SEE ITS RESULTS.

- ♦ FAITH IS NOT ADMITTING THERE IS A GOD BUT TRUSTING HIM WITH YOUR TOTAL LIFE.

- ♦ THERE IS LITTLE FAITH, FAITH, AND GREAT FAITH, THAT CORRESPONDS TO NOT ENOUGH, JUST ENOUGH, AND MORE THAN ENOUGH.

FIFTEEN

SAL MISTRY

COURAGE TO
ACCEPT IDENTITY

Men need not pray for opportunities,
but pray to be ready when opportunities come.

Sal never finished anything he started. But even he felt a little ashamed when he came home after a year at college without earning any credits toward a degree. Braced for the recrimination of his mother, Zuby, he was shocked when she said nothing. Instead, Zuby stood up for him against her family's anger and defended Sal's right to go to work without a college education. Sal didn't realize that he was dealing with a changed mother, and her change would ultimately send him on an odyssey into Christ and back to his heritage.

Zuby was born in East Africa and raised in Pakistan, where she met and married a handsome Indian. They were Muslims of the Ismaili sect who followed the Aga Khan, Shah Karim. Leaving Pakistan, the couple moved to London, where Saleem and Salman were born. Shortly after the boys' births, they moved to Toronto, Canada, and divorced. Zuby took her sons to Texas, where her family had built a motel business.

Texas was a good place for them. Zuby's father and brother made a place for her in their motel business, which led her ten years later into opening her own restaurant in Dallas. Saleem received fatherly input and advice from his uncle and grandfather and grew up as a normal Texas kid. Growing up in the West, Saleem shortened his name to Sal, rebuffed any religious or cultural heritage his mother tried to give him, and adopted western culture as his own. That included becoming a self-proclaimed "party animal," who was out to find the most amount of fun, with the most amount of people, for the most amount of time.

Education was critically important to Zuby and her family. Pressed to attend college, Sal looked for schools out of state to get away from family and influences that might restrain his appetite for pleasure. As he traveled to scout out schools, the sight of a beautiful woman in a bikini top riding her bike across campus convinced him that Arizona State was the place for him. He enrolled and found his way into a fraternity with a Christian origin. Although none of the young men actually followed the faith, Sal learned something about Jesus Christ in the fraternity ceremonies and felt good that it was one more "white" thing he could do to separate himself from his cultural heritage. But while Sal partied in Arizona, Zuby met God in Texas.

One day a salesman had called on her to sell her a restaurant ad in a Christian yellow page directory. "You have to be a Christian to advertise with us," he said.

"What is that?" she asked. She had been attending church with her boyfriend, Mike, who insisted she go, even though he wasn't leading a Christian life at the time. In her Muslim sect, it didn't matter if you attended another church, so long as you also went to the Jamatkhana to worship. She liked what Mike's church preached, but she didn't know what it meant to be Christian, and his lifestyle only left her confused.

"I've gone to church a few times," she told the salesman, "does that make me a Christian?"

"Look," the man said, pointing to the "sinner's prayer" written at the bottom of a form he handed her, "you have to say that prayer out loud and sign the form that you are a Christian, then you can advertise with us."

Zuby was horrified at first. Her family would disown her if she did such a thing. They tolerated other religions, but you could not turn your back on your Muslim faith or heritage. But then she figured no one would ever find out, and she could use the advertising. So she took the paper, said the prayer out loud, signed the form, and bought the ad. She didn't know exactly what happened, but she felt somehow different after that.

A few months later, as she listened to the Christian radio station in her car that her boyfriend Mike had tuned in, she made a full commitment to Christ. Delirious with excitement, Zuby called her family and told them the good news — not only was Jesus alive, but He was alive in Zuby! Enraged, they rejected her outright. She was undeterred, and called her sons to tell them as well.

"Saleem?" the voice came over the phone. "I need to tell you I've changed. I'm a Christian."

Sal was happy to hear from his mother. The fraternity had influenced his life, but he didn't understand exactly that his mother had experienced a total life change. Thinking she had just found some new western cultural awareness, he said, "I've changed too, Mama."

"You're not mad at me that I'm Christian?" she asked eagerly.

"No, Mama, that's fine with me," he assured her.

Sal continued his year of parties and binges, then came home to a woman he'd never met — his mother. Zuby had prayed for her boys, and God had already assured her they would be saved. Instead of the usual pressure about college and anger about the year he'd blown, Sal was shocked when his mother simply said, "You do what you want, Saleem, and it's going to work out fine."

Sal finally enrolled near home at the University of North Texas. Frat houses still held more interest than the classroom, and he excelled there, becoming rush chairman and finally president — always coming up with more outrageous pranks, stunts, or parties. He quit school for jobs and jobs for school, always justifying in his own mind quitting what he started. Yet nothing satisfied. He was lusting for something and loving nothing. After five years of higher education in two universities, Sal was still unfinished and incomplete in school. He was frustrated at the emptiness he felt and saw in the fraternity, as well as in himself.

"Mama, I just don't get it," he said one day, pouring his heart out at a coffee shop with Zuby.

"We had a guy die in a drunk driving accident in our fraternity, and the guys are still driving drunk. I've talked to them, made speeches, and tried to tell them where we're wrong, but they won't listen to me. Why can't I change them?"

"Because you're using the wrong person," Zuby counseled her son. "You can't change anyone. Only Jesus Christ can."

Sal's mother's prayers prevailed against his pattern. A week later he attended a home Bible study and repeated the "sinner's prayer" his mother had read off an advertising form. Within two years, Sal had the privilege of leading his brother to Christ. And Zuby married Mike, who was magnificently reunited with Christ; and the family was united in one faith.

Months later, Sal left school once again to pursue a job that would take him around the world as an aide to a minister. As he ministered, the Holy Spirit ministered to him. Sal realized the angry resentment he had toward his dad for not being there as he grew up. He released his father's sins through forgiveness, then realized his life had followed his father's pattern — going from job to job, never completing what he started. With forgiveness freeing him from that lifestyle, seven months later Sal made a decision. He received the blessings of his mother, employer, and pastor, and went back to school.

The strident pace of both school and work kept Sal busy, and many times he wanted to quit. But within nine months he completed the course work and graduated admirably, with high grades and a proud family behind him. But the education he received was nothing compared to breaking the curse off his life. His diploma was a testimony that for the first time in his life, Sal finished something.

But there was much more to come. On a ministry trip to Africa, in an afternoon service, he became deeply convicted. He closed his eyes tightly, but couldn't stop the tears from spilling over. As he prayed, he saw a mental image of an Indian woman and young Indian boy with fire under their feet. Sal realized he had always been ashamed of the color of his skin, and because of that, the people of his Indian and Pakistan heritage were dying without the message of Christ's saving grace he could bring them. Returning home two weeks later, Sal went to his mother first to ask for forgiveness.

"I'm sorry Mama," he said through tears. "I was always ashamed of our skin, our culture, everything about the way God made us. I was wrong. I didn't realize He had a purpose for it — that I'm exactly who He needs me to be."

"I always knew, Saleem," Zuby said, "but I didn't know how to tell you. I'm so happy now."

On another trip, this time to Mexico, he listened to a message about men's relationships, and the story of a pastor who sought forgiveness from every woman he'd had relations with outside of marriage. Sal was almost sweating as he searched his heart and said, "God, if you ask me to do the same, I will."

That evening as he prayed, he knew God was requiring of him the same standard He'd required of that pastor. As soon as he returned home, Sal picked up the telephone and started calling old girlfriends. He felt ashamed and embarrassed, but each call was met with a friendly thank you, and one by one, he felt released of all those old relationships.

Now purified of the past, with a picture of what his future might hold, Sal was eager to move on with all God had for him. The next thing he felt God lead him to was a trip to India — the last place he'd ever considered going. He went to churches and friends to raise support and started faxing and e-mailing contacts in India. After completing all the arrangements, he left on a three-week mission trip to India with a full schedule to minister to pastors, leaders, and especially young people. As he ministered the few messages he'd prepared, hundreds of young adults repented of sexual immorality and made the same vow he made, to be pure before God until marriage. Hundreds of pastors, amazed at the young man's faith, repented of disunity and pledged to work together to reach young men for Christ.

While there, Sal discovered that his heritage, his sect, gave him access to reach every person in India's rigid caste system. Such entree came only by birth, not by choice. It became clear why God had brought him to the point of accepting his culture so dramatically. As he talked with pastors and leaders, he learned that people around the world were praying for at least one man in the Aga Khan social system to come to know Jesus Christ. Sal accepted the responsibility to be that man.

Today Sal continues to serve in ministry, believing that as he is faithful in another man's ministry and is obedient to what God asks of him each day, God will give Sal his own ministry, and the dream he has of his future will become a reality.

It took courage for Sal to stand up and accept responsibility. It took courage for Sal to accept himself, and even more courage to act on who he was. But that's what Sal is now — a man of decisive action.

Sal came to me in a most unusual way. As a new Christian, he heard a teaching on "mentoring" and prayed that God would give him the mentor he never had, being raised in a fatherless home. Relatives provided male influence, but the absence of a father left a vacuum in his manhood. He was challenged during a church conference to make a list of those he would most like to have mentor him, and Edwin Louis

Cole was at the top of his list. Believing that to be impossible, he sought direction elsewhere. He attended an early morning Bible study with his singles pastor and told him about an opportunity to move away and work with a minister he highly respected.

"Why don't you wait about a week and just fast and pray on that," the singles pastor recommended. Sal agreed.

A week later, a Christian Men's Network executive committee agreed somebody needed to travel with me full time. Our events manager was appointed to find candidates. His first call was to an associate pastor of a nearby church — Sal's church. The associate met the singles pastor in a hallway that morning and asked if he knew someone who would be good for the job.

"Yes, I think I do. Let me get back to you on that," the singles pastor replied.

"How would you like to travel with Edwin Louis Cole?" he asked Sal the next morning when they met.

"What?" Sal asked, shocked. A few phone calls and four interviews later, Sal was retained as my personal assistant. Since then, he has traveled around two-thirds of the world with me, and on his own.

Sal immersed himself in the teaching of the ministry. Viewing a video entitled, "Released," he became aware of his father's sins being retained in his life through unforgiveness. Forgiveness freed him from it all and made it possible for him to talk to his father for the first time.

Sal says today, "It amazed me that in one act of obedience, cycles in my life were broken, generational curses removed, and old patterns became new ones."

One step of obedience led to another, and then came India. Sal's story of his trip to India is a prime example of the truth that men need not pray for opportunities, but pray to be ready when opportunities come. God is going to bring opportunities your way, but will you be ready to act on them? It took courage for Sal to act.

"In the natural I had many things working against me," Sal said recently. "I was not a seasoned minister, knew no one in India, and had no money. But I knew that 'dreams are the substance of every great achievement in life.' That truth gave me the courage to believe I could go to India and actually make a difference. God provided the contacts, money, and time, and I had the greatest three weeks of my life."

What qualifies Sal as a man of courage is that it takes courage to admit who we are and accept our identity. An identity crisis is ever the initial and continuing critical issue in a man's life. Men identify themselves by the amount of money they make, the clothes or uniform they wear, the house they live in, or the employer for whom they work. Accepting themselves for who they are, submitting to it, and letting it become a strength is vital.

God knew that.

Jesus said, *Whosoever therefore shall confess me before men, him will I confess also before my Father which is in heaven* (Matthew 10:32). Identification with Jesus Christ here and now is mandatory for Him to identify with us then and there for our entry into heaven.

Men who lack the courage to confess and identify with Christ now will suffer from the lack of going to heaven later. Embarrassed to be called Christian, afraid to suffer the indignity the world heaps upon those who bear His name, the poltroon in his poltroonery will spend a Christless eternity tormented by the memory of what he lacked in faith and courage — the challenge to identify with Christ.

Poltroon? It means a spiritless coward!

Former friends may call Sal strange, but he just changed the kind of party he attended. He's preparing for the ultimate party in heaven.

Party now, or party then. It's your choice.

P R I N C I P L E S *for* COURAGEOUS MANHOOD

♦ MEN NEED NOT PRAY FOR OPPORTUNITIES, BUT PRAY TO BE READY WHEN THEY COME.

♦ DREAMS ARE THE SUBSTANCE OF EVERY GREAT ACHIEVEMENT IN LIFE.

SIXTEEN

A. R. BERNARD

COURAGE TO
SET PRIORITIES

*You must not sacrifice your family
on the altar of your career or ministry.*

How could he not give the man the money? Al stood for a minute, wavering between the needs of his family and the needs of the unkempt man he was ministering to on a sidewalk in the projects of New York. The man said his car was broken and he needed some money to buy the parts so he could get to work and wouldn't lose his job. Al pulled his hand out of his pocket and peeled off a few bills from a thin roll for the man. It would mean Al couldn't buy his family the groceries they needed, but he figured they would somehow get by until his next paycheck. They always did.

Al came home to find that his pregnant wife had been hospitalized. Karen was usually a laugh a minute — a spunky, spontaneous, wisecracking young woman. She was so full of life that her charms outweighed all Al's resistance, and he had plunged into a love for her that he had vowed would be life-long on the day they married.

"The doctor says I'm under too much stress," Karen told him when he walked into her hospital room. "I couldn't wait for you. I had to go to the doctor."

Al felt terrible that he hadn't been there for Karen. He was torn between attending to his wife and fulfilling God's call on his life to minister. He wanted to go out and do the ministry he loved so well, then come home to a happy wife and a peaceful home, not to more of the problems he'd just been solving.

Al's ministry was still a part-time venture at that time, an "on-call," all-service helps ministry squeezed into the free hours after work and on weekends, around his regular job at the bank. When someone called, he came running. His love for God and thankfulness for being saved from a desperate life of sin motivated him to go to the highways and byways of life to tell everyone, "Jesus loves you, He forgives, and He'll make a way for you."

The doctor told Al that Karen's blood pressure had spiked sharply. She was suffering from carrying a bit more than what a young mother could bear. Al saw it as a way for the devil to steal his time in ministry — another way Satan was trying to keep him from doing the Lord's work. He prayed fervently for Karen, and eventually the pregnancy brought a wonderful baby — his firstborn son, Alfonso.

One more brother joined baby Alfonso with another on the way when Al went into full-time ministry, starting a church in a storefront that had begun as a Bible study with just himself, Karen, and their tiny boys. As the church grew, so did the demands on Al's time. He knew he had to be there for his congregation, because that's what pastoring was all about — being the man, the friend, the counselor, the advisor, and still having enough time to study the Word and be the preacher on Sundays.

The people didn't see Karen much, or seem to think much of her at the church. Because Al didn't give her first priority, they didn't either. Karen resigned herself to third or fourth place in Al's life. She'd just raise the kids and be content with that. Although she determined to bear it, the stress was constantly increasing.

Two more brothers joined the first three. The church grew exponentially at the same time, and Al found his days full, his nights busy, and his weekends a nonstop whirlwind as he prepared and gave the messages God gave him for the people. He had almost no time for anything at home.

Karen attended most church services, getting all five boys ready along with a teenage helper, making sure they were dressed right and arrived on time, and tending to them alone as Al tended to the rest of the flock. Her next pregnancy caused her considerable stress once again. Again Al prayed for her fervently, trying to fight the devil, and wanting the problems at home to go away so he could be free to do the ministry to which God had called him.

But their sixth child miscarried. Karen couldn't handle the pregnancy with the heavy load she carried. Resentful of Al's uncaring attitude toward her, she withdrew — angry, isolated, a single mom with a husband on the side. Al resented her anger and believed a separation from her might be the only solution. For all appearances, she already felt divorced.

Al pressed on, keeping a busy church calendar and attending conferences to continue increasing the ministry. Dr. Cho of South Korea was the featured speaker at a luncheon at a pastor's conference Al attended. He had left Karen at home with the kids and checked into the hotel, excited to learn all that these great leaders had to offer at the conference. The lunchroom was buzzing with preachers and their "preacher talk," and Al felt right at home, happy to be in the fellowship of his brethren. But as Dr. Cho spoke, he began to touch areas of Al's life that had nothing to do with church growth, sermons, or strategic planning.

What Al heard was a startling confession. The way he remembers it, Dr. Cho said that he thought his wife's demands were the result of Western thought encroaching on their lives. "I needed to be a true husband to her, as Christ is to the Church."

Reeling from the confrontation with truth, Al went to the rest of the meetings that day stone-faced, then retreated to his hotel room. The next day he didn't leave. Laying on his hotel room floor, crying out to God, he came to grips with his part in the situation at home. He realized that he was responsible. He was responsible for Karen's attitude, her stress, the people's lack of respect for her, and ultimately, for the death of their unborn child. He collapsed under the weight of it, unable to reconcile in his mind what atonement could possibly be made, what he could possibly do to rectify the situation. For six hours he lay there praying, pleading with God for forgiveness, asking for direction of some kind. He knew he was guilty — he had sacrificed his family for the sake of his ministry, losing perspective by ignoring priorities.

As he released all that was within him, God began to replace the old with the new. He showed Al that he would have to repent to Karen, but that he couldn't expect Karen to respond right away. Al received assurance deep within that if he lived out his decisions and did not just talk about them, things would change. The issue for Al was to correct his priorities as God pointed him to the truth, and to walk in the truth God gave.

Al arose from the floor and dialed his home telephone number. A weary Karen answered. Al repented to her and asked for her forgiveness. Her flat, dull voice confirmed to him what God had already warned. When he returned home, he began to study the manhood of Jesus Christ, to find out what it really meant to be a man. If being a man didn't mean being the best at what you did for work and becoming successful in what you attempted, then where was the glory of being a man? As he studied, he realized the glory that came from being a husband and father first, setting his own house in order before trying to solve everyone else's problems. He learned that when he thought he'd been fighting the devil, it was often his own ignorance he was up against.

Once Al was no longer caught up in the busy life of church activities, once he began to counsel less and teach his people to pray more, once he gave away less money and taught his church body proper stewardship, God began to lead him down paths he never expected. Karen once again became the funny, perky woman that lit up his life. She birthed her sixth baby boy in 1988, when the church had about 500 members. Since then, she and Al have brought in three more teenage boys to nurture and raise.

With the home fully nurtured, the church started to grow. By 1990, Al had 1000 members in church, and in 1996 his church topped 3000 members. Concentrating on teaching men what God had taught him about manhood, he built an infrastructure that perpetuates itself, with men teaching men, and congregation members being served by others, which frees him to study the Word and stay ahead of the flock he's leading.

❧

The next time I saw him after our first meeting, I did not know him. At our first meeting, he was not the master of martial arts he is now. Out of shape and overweight, it was obvious that his was a congregation that knew how to cook. I remember that we did not meet again for several years, and when we did, I didn't recognize him. Slim, trim, athletic, militant in demeanor, disciplined in deportment, he was the antithesis of my memory of him.

His keen mind had become that of a student. He mentally digested everything said, metabolized it, incorporated it into his philosophy, kept what was profitable, and threw away the rest. He had no room for the nonessentials.

As he disciplined himself to nurture his wife and children first, he grew in stature with God and man and so did his ministry and congregation. His only desire was to share the good news of Jesus Christ, the Gospel that had rescued him from a life of distractions and emptiness. Almost shipwrecked by his zeal, God's mercy corrrected him and saved him from an age-old blunder — sacrificing your family on the altar of your career or ministry. A fatherless child, born out of wedlock, of mixed parentage, his frustration was understandable. But Jesus changed all that. He gave him meaning, purpose, and a way of life that was both satisfying and challenging.

He wanted adventure in his life. Jesus gave it to him.

He wanted maturity in his manhood. Jesus gave it to him.

He wanted a good family life. Jesus gave it to him.

He wanted to be a leader, not a follower. Jesus made him one.

On the verge of making a terrible mistake, God arrested him. Then he found the book *Maximized Manhood*. It was what he was looking for — someone or something to get him started on what it was to be a man — to stop him from thinking divorce and to encourage him to take responsibility for his own actions.

It was my privilege to know him in those early days when you had to walk upstairs to get to the little hall to worship. So small and tight was the stairway, you had to stand against the side wall to let others pass. People lined up to get in then, as they do now, only now they line up around the block and wait for hours to worship.

In those early days, the struggle to grow, the passion for preaching, the need for financing, and the ever present concern for a wife and six boys was a juggling act of time, attention, and industry. It was all work at church and at home. He learned through God's grace that he could not sacrifice his family in the process.

That was the sin of Eli, the prophet in the Old Testament. His sons made themselves vile and he "restrained them not." God cut off his posterity, telling Eli he honored his sons more than Him by allowing them to desecrate the worship in the Temple. (See 1 Samuel 2.) God still holds the father accountable for his sons' conduct. When the pastor changed to become "father" first, the home changed.

I remember one funny incident when his son, who had outgrown him, made a comment that he could whip his dad. They were standing in the kitchen, and the boy had a spoon in his hand to eat some ice cream. Hearing his son's comment, his father used a martial arts kick to knock the spoon out of the boy's hand and catch it in midair so fast, it turned his son's complexion pale. None of the others have ever said such a thing.

He had been guilty of a common sin that many men overlook. Of the five sins that kept Israel from entering Canaan after leaving Egypt, idolatry was the first. Idolatry is defined as a devotion to anything in priority to devotion to God. Some ministers and men make their ministry or career an idol. Their affinity and affection for their work takes precedence over family and even intimacy with God. But what satisfies and fulfills him in his vocation does little to provide the same for his family. A divorced wife and rebellious children are but two of the terrible consequences.

Karen has acquired a natural "down-home" wisdom through the experience of the six-plus-three sons and a congregation of thousands. Her sense of humor is fully restored and something I can always count on when I call. I remember the day my distraught daughter called her for advice about her fifteen-year-old son.

"Karen, you've raised all those boys," Joann said. "How do you deal with them? How do you know what they're thinking?"

Karen answered in her quick, lively, and penetrating fashion, "Boys don't think!"

That settled it for Joann. She never again asked her sons, "What were you thinking?"

The last big episode I heard about from Karen was their adventures with a new family dog her husband brought home. "He must have got that dog from the 'hood," Karen said, "because he's got no manners! He doesn't behave, won't learn anything, and does whatever he wants!"

Now they laugh as a couple about things that were deadly serious years ago. Living through life's difficulties and distresses converted most of their experiences into laughable, pleasant memories later. Recalling them illustrates the means by which they were bonded together into family unity. Scars are the visible evidence of a hurt that has healed.

"Be of good courage" means to be of God's courage. Good courage produces God's kind of men and women.

Now the boys are growing and marrying. Karen is getting the wedding she always wanted on their twenty-fifth anniversary. It will be an all-out, full-blown ceremony with the gown she didn't have the first time, and a honeymoon that is more than a weekend out of town. Their lives are full, lively, industrious, and productive. And he is no longer Al, but "Dr. A. R. Bernard," a man of great courage.

PRINCIPLES *for* COURAGEOUS MANHOOD

♦ YOU MUST NOT SACRIFICE YOUR FAMILY ON THE ALTAR OF YOUR CAREER OR MINISTRY.

SEVENTEEN

BRUCE BINKLEY

COURAGE TO RISK

Peace is the umpire for knowing the will of God.

"I'd like a tent-making business," Bruce told Kevin as they drove toward a men's event one summer day. "I'd like to be able to support myself, instead of being on the payroll of a ministry. And I've always had it in my heart to give, but I don't have much that I can give."

"Well then," Kevin said, "let's just pray about that right now."

The two men agreed in prayer that Bruce would find a tent-making business that would allow him to provide for his family, minister, and give to missions. He always wanted to be a big giver, but his salary didn't allow it. And he'd always heard incredible stories of people who "proved" God by giving — Wesley, Penney, LeTourneau — something he'd never experienced himself.

At the time, Bruce was working full-time for a Christian ministry. Being on the payroll of a ministry wasn't his dream, but to launch out not knowing where he could possibly land would be a big step of faith. He told his wife Camella what was on his heart. It wasn't until four years later, at his cousin's lake house, that they motored out to the middle of the lake at sunset one night and prayed, "God, give us a business that we can run together, will be profitable, will provide for our family, will help people, and will allow us to minister and give to fulfill what you've placed in our hearts."

The next year, Bruce resigned his ministry position and went to a cabin at a nearby lake to have a meeting with God alone. He took his pen, some paper, his Bible, a few bottles of water, and his dog. He didn't know how long he'd be gone, but he was serious about not making a move until it was what God wanted for him and his family.

"God, what do You want me to do?" he asked seriously.

No answer came, so Bruce continued to fast and pray all day. He had heard about a business opportunity in the personnel staffing industry, and as his mind wandered, he mulled it over. He could get a government loan to buy the company, he'd be working to help people, he and Camella could work together, and if they did well, they would be successful financially. It was too bad that it involved moving away, otherwise it sounded good.

Another night passed in the cabin and Bruce still heard nothing, and saw no signs. But the more he thought about the personnel staffing business, the better he liked the idea. Being without a job, he knew the pressure unemployed people experienced, so it would be rewarding work if he could get jobless people on their feet again. He grew peaceful and confident that he and Camella could run it, but he still waited to hear from God.

On the third afternoon, Bruce was getting hungry when he thought of the principle, "Peace is the umpire for knowing the will of God." He realized he hadn't heard anything directly, but he did have peace. He thought he was waiting on God, but he began to wonder if God might not be waiting on him.

He drove home singing and immediately told Camella his idea. The only problem remaining was that to qualify for the loan, he needed to have $30,000 in the bank. Working in ministry left him with less than one-hundredth that amount. He made a few calls to people who came to mind, and told them his plans, never asking for money. After four calls, he had $36,000 pledged to help him. The next good news was that a franchise close to home was for sale. It had existing customers and positive cash flow, and cost the same as a new franchise. Without even having to relocate, he and Camella bought it, their first franchise.

The business started to grow right away. The only person who stayed with the office soon quit, and he and Camella put in sixteen-hour days to keep it running. Determined to be givers, they tithed off the gross from the first day they opened. By the next fall, they were doing very well financially, and God spoke to Bruce about giving more. To give more, Bruce needed more, so in November they invested in another franchise of the same business and opened a second office.

As they set their goals for the coming year, Bruce remembered something he'd heard years earlier — that you could "tithe" by faith, based on what you trusted God to make, not based on what you had already made. He and Camella set their plans for what they desired to earn the next year, and in January they started tithing off their goals, not their gross. The first tithe check Bruce wrote was staggering — 50 percent of their total gross income. But even after tithing, they managed to pay every bill.

By September of that year, they reached their goal and the tithe check he wrote was for only 10 percent of their gross income that month. It seemed as though they'd been given a big raise with the extra money from the increased income, since the tithe check was now only 10 percent of the gross instead of 50 percent, so they joyfully increased their offerings instead. At the end of the year, he and Camella set their goals for what they wanted to earn the following year once again, and they started writing out those tithe checks.

A desire of Bruce's heart, mentioned to a friend in a car, turned into a profitable business that has more than met every need he spelled out to the Lord. Bruce and Camella don't work the long hours anymore, except for the occasional crisis, and they see no limit in view for what God might have for them next as He gently leads them by giving them peace.

Bruce knew the principle that peace is the umpire for knowing the will of God. Acting on the peace he felt, he needed no external signs, set no "fleece" before God to determine His will, and sought no more counsel except the confirmation of friends whom God brought to his mind — those who ended up loaning him the money to get started.

This is principle-based living. I've taught men all over the world that the more you live your life on principle, the straighter will be your course and the greater will be your life. But the more you live your life on personality, living by the dictates of circumstances and personal opinion, the more difficult will be your course and life. Bruce acted on the principles, and they served him well.

Bruce learned the principles while we worked together in the ministry. It was Bruce who was my classic example of the difference between being "called" and "hired." Bruce came to minister with me after working as a salesman in the insurance business. He had been with us four years when our income took a sharp drop and I did not know how we could keep paying everyone. At that time, he and I were ministering in a conference being held in a hotel in Niagara Falls. Early that Thursday morning, as we sat in a coffee shop for breakfast, I informed him of my decision to let him go — sever him — dismiss him. By the time I was through, we were both in tears.

The following Monday morning, back at the office in Dallas, Bruce was sitting in his usual place working. I avoided entering his office for an hour. Finally getting up the courage, I went and stood in his doorway.

"Bruce," I said, "I know you understood me, because we both agreed on it. So why are you still here?"

"I'll tell you why," Bruce said emphatically. "You didn't hire me, God called me. If God called me, then you can't fire me!"

To argue with that, I would have had to argue with God, and I wasn't about to do that. In the next two weeks he showed me how imperative it was to have him where he was. As the finances came back up, not only did Bruce stay, but I gave him a raise. In jest, I informed everybody I would never try to fire him again — I couldn't afford the raise!

Bruce was right. God-called men are divinely planted where they are. To touch them is to touch God's anointed, as much as touching an anointed minister.

Bruce is working with us again as a layman, giving generously of his time, talent, and treasury. Years before beginning his own business, it took courage added to his faith to come back to the office and work with no indication of ever being paid for it. That single act, in my estimation, was a seed sown that is producing the results in his business today.

Bruce hasn't just learned the principles of courageous manhood, he practices them — daily! His has not been a charmed life. A painful divorce while he worked with me made him feel less than qualified to teach other men. God had to do a work within Bruce, going all the way back to his childhood. Bruce allowed Him to do it, painful as it often was. But he learned, he's still learning, and his lessons are paying off.

So here we are. Think about it. Are you called or hired at your work, business, or ministry? Do you have peace of heart about what you're doing? If not, why not?

Act now.

If it's a cabin getaway you need, do it. If it's an apology you must make, pick up the phone. If it's a job you must leave, write the letter now. If it's a business you must start, tomorrow is too late. Seek God. Get His peace for your life. Then live in that peace, practicing His principles, moving ever forward in courageous manhood.

P R I N C I P L E S *for* COURAGEOUS MANHOOD

♦ PEACE IS THE UMPIRE FOR KNOWING THE WILL OF GOD.

- THE MORE YOU LIVE YOUR LIFE ON PRINCIPLE, THE STRAIGHTER WILL BE YOUR COURSE AND THE GREATER WILL BE YOUR LIFE.

- WERE YOU CALLED OR HIRED? IF GOD CALLS YOU, THEN YOU CAN'T BE FIRED.

EIGHTEEN

DAVID MCKENZIE

COURAGE TO DESTROY AN IMAGE

The most powerful thing you can do in life is to create an image.
The next most powerful thing is to destroy an image.

"God, what is wrong here?" Barbara demanded. "What is going on? What's wrong with my husband?"

Barbara knew she had a rocky marriage, but there was something more to it that she sensed, and she couldn't understand. She'd married David after knowing him in high school, then meeting him in church later. He was fun, exciting, handsome — everything she'd dreamed of. When they married, people said it was a perfect match. But when trouble came, Barbara found herself alone on the deck of her home with her Bible, seeking a way out, daily entreating the God of her youth for solutions. She never suspected what she was about to find out, and she never dreamed that God's solutions would completely change everything she and David knew or thought about life.

David grew up in a happy, middle-class home with siblings and parents who loved each other, even if his father had a hard time expressing it. But when his mother suddenly died as he turned twelve, his grieving father couldn't see any way of raising the youngest children still at home without their mother. He sent David to live with a relative for a summer. While there, David found an escape from his grief and loneliness in his relative's pornographic magazines. The images created in his mind would serve to haunt him later. Coming from a respectable family, the relative thought nothing of continuing in the habit patterns of his highly successful father, which included subscriptions to pornographic magazines. He thought it was normal, just something men do.

When David returned to his home, it was to an erratic father who had started drinking heavily and flew into drunken rages. For a brief time, David's father sent him and his little sister to stay in a children's home. When David threatened to run away from the home months later, he was welcomed back to his father's house, but their relationship was strained.

Smart and ambitious, David dropped out of sports during high school and began to work, starting in manual labor and, after graduating from college, at a sales job with a paving company. Out on the road in his company car, without a schedule or anyone looking over his shoulder, he found comfort and companionship in the images of pornographic magazines once again. The paving business was full of rowdy, rough-hewn men who encouraged David to dabble in pornography.

Marrying his sweet wife, Barbara, and having three wonderful baby boys, David found himself incapable and uneducated in loving as a husband and father. He flew into angry rages with his family, just like his dad had with him, then retreated into the magazines that put no demands on him. They gave him a false sense of intimacy, and that left him no room to be intimate with his family.

David saw his wife growing desperate, trying to be a good wife to an angry husband and to make a home for their three small boys. When God revealed to Barbara that the problem was pornography, she sought help. The pastors at their church didn't talk about such things, and no one was available to help, so unbeknownst to David, she grabbed her Bible daily as her sons napped and went out on her deck to find God. God met her there.

David was taken aback and enraged when Barbara took a firm stand, telling him he'd have to leave if the pornography continued. A little worried at his wife's resolve, David acted the way she wanted him to act, but he was addicted to the images in his mind. Then came the men's meetings, to which Barbara accompanied him for moral support. The challenge David received at the meetings made him aware of how inadequate he really was, and that made him feel worse. He controlled his anger, hoping to stay with his wife longer.

Then came counseling with specialized professionals who enraged David. He came home fuming, but the stirring inside was beginning to shake his love for the images in his mind. For Barbara, nothing seemed to change at home, but she began to see what God had in store for her husband. She caught a vision of who David really was and pressed into God in prayer, believing for that vision to become a reality.

David took each step like a spoonful of medicine, hating it, yet agreeing to it because he knew deep within that something had to change. He did his part, and God did His. When confronted with his secret habit, David fought to free himself from it, but alternately embraced it stronger. He saw its destructive nature, yet was unwilling to let go of the solace it provided. Three different times he threw out all the pornography in the house, only to replace it again later.

While this struggle continued, he was confronted with another issue — the bitter resentment he felt toward his father. When David recognized his need to forgive his father, the deliverance process started. Within the process of forgiveness came an ability to let go of the old images in his mind. David released his grip on pornography and started to retreat from rage. His efforts brought great results at home. Barbara was no longer on his back, and his children began to respond to him with love, not fear. David liked the feeling that gave him. Over the course of a few years, a new image of himself, his life, his purpose, and his destiny in God replaced the old, and his former lifestyle ceased to exist.

When the old images were replaced with the new, everything changed. David was soon asked to give his testimony at a prison program. Then he was asked to teach the principles of *Maximized Manhood* at a youth correctional facility. They gave him a weekly Bible study with the young men, aged eighteen to twenty-one, who were within twelve months of being released.

"Listen up so you know what you're gonna face out there," David said boldly. "You're gonna get out there and fall flat on your butt and end up back here again unless you learn what I'm gonna teach you. I can't do nothing for you but show you the way. It's up to you to go there."

David's unpolished presentation attracted the young men's attention. After his opening statements, he played a men's teaching video, stopping it from time to time to tell them how he applied the truth to his own life. The young men listened intently, knowing that it wasn't a program — it was real life.

Even though going to the prison once a week sometimes put a strain on family time, Barbara agreed to it. She realized later that by sowing into others, the seeds of truth were changing her husband even more. Over a few year's time, David's heart softened toward his sons and he no longer had to work as hard to control his temper — he simply didn't want to blow up at them anymore. In his heart, by God's guidance, he was becoming a real father.

And the results in the prison were dramatic. Young killers turned their lives to Jesus. David saw the hold pornography had on almost the entire prison population and was able to speak to them boldly about its dangers.

Then came the breakthroughs financially. David went to a conference where they talked about faith, giving, and stewardship. The men talked about the teaching among themselves during breaks.

"David," a friend said to him, "I believe God is ministering to me about the Year of Jubilee."

"What's that?" David asked.

"It's from the Old Testament. Every forty-nine years, the Israelites canceled all their debts. I believe God's going to get me out of debt, even my house mortgage."

David went home excited. "Barbara, we're going to get completely out of debt. This is the year." Barbara was shocked, so David prayed until God brought her into agreement with him.

Years earlier, David had borrowed money from his father to start his own paving business. The principle that you are the servant to the lender seemed to put even more pressure on their relationship, which made it more difficult for David to feel accepted by his father. Business was somewhat steady, but always provided only enough to keep the lights on and the children clothed. David had bought new equipment along the way with bank loans and paid the monthly minimums regularly. But now they had an entirely new mind-set. They earnestly prayed for God to show them a way.

"I believe we need to take 10 percent of what we owe on the house and business and give it to ministry," Barbara told David one night. "That's just what I think God is saying to me."

David agreed. He had learned by this time that it was obedience to God that would protect him and his family. He'd had every opportunity to stray, or return to his former ways, but the fear of the Lord kept him. In obedience to what they believed God said, by faith they wrote a check out of their business that equaled 10 percent of the total business debt. Barbara pondered how they could come up with 10 percent of the total they owed on their house, which was their only other debt. As she juggled their personal budget, she found that by going without and paring down to the very lowest standard of living possible, they could, over a few months, give to the church building program exactly 10 percent of what they owed on their house. She and David agreed, and they did it.

By this time David had gone back to both his father and brother and asked for forgiveness. Only months after making peace within the family, David's father suddenly died. The brothers were united at the funeral and could bury their father without regret. When the estate was settled, David and Barbara received just enough money to pay off every debt their business had. A load lifted from them emotionally, spiritually, and physically.

David didn't understand how it happened, but it seemed as if the weight of debt on his business lifted, and a door that had been barred shut before opened. New jobs began to come his way. When he landed two big jobs, he and Barbara took all the profits and paid off their house mortgage entirely. Within twelve months, they were entirely debt free. It was impossible, but God made the way for them.

David's desire to give has not stopped, and the pattern God has given him and Barbara has continued. When their oldest son entered college, they felt God tell them to give away the funds they had saved for college. They did it, then wondered if they were foolish parents for not providing for their son's education. When scholarships started pouring in, Barbara went back to check the records. The amount they had saved and given away was exactly 10 percent of what they needed for Justin's four years at school. With two years left, Justin has a credit balance on his account at college, and God continues to provide supernaturally for him.

Today Barbara says she wanted to stick her head in the sand in those early, awful years. She really didn't want to know the truth and would rather have run from the terrible situation she was in. But she believes God gave her the vision He has for David, and the courage to stand against the wrong and for the right. That vision is still unfolding, and all she has to do is make a stand, pray, and give God enough time to see it come about.

David says he simply is not the same man. He is well-known in the community today. Keeping the covenants he made with God, his wife, his sons, and others, he has grown into an outstanding man of God. After fourteen years of prison ministry, he has the respect of the state governor and has been appointed to several local and state prison boards. He is revered by his banker, his vendors, and the rough-and-tumble ex-cons to whom he gives jobs and training. He took his family out of a church that was powerless to help them and moved them to a Bible-believing church where they are pillars of strength and stability. Best of all, David is loved and respected by his beautiful wife and admired by his growing sons.

❖

The most powerful thing we can do in life is create an image. Images in the mind occupy our thoughts. Our thoughts shape our beliefs. Our beliefs influence our decisions. Our decisions affect our actions. Our actions determine our destiny.

The next most powerful thing we can do is to destroy an image. Once David's mental images changed, his entire life changed. What began as an innocent curiosity about something that appeared "manly" became a snare that kept David's mind in bondage and destroyed his ability to function in the truly "manly" roles God had placed him.

When I first met David McKenzie, he was a far cry from the man I spoke to on his cellular phone recently, talking loudly and happily, in answer to my question as to where he was.

"I'm in my car driving down the highway, living in Christ's victory, celebrating His 'Year of Jubilee' in my life. What can I do for you?"

"How's business?" I asked him.

"I bought out the competition. I've cornered the market! And I'm debt free!" he answered happily. The funny thing is, I know the man who told him about the Year of Jubilee, and he's still paying off his house!

My first meeting with David was in a high school auditorium in Washington, D.C. He was leaning against a wall, his wife standing anxiously nearby, and looking at me quizzically. How could I know his life was badly messed up — a condition of his own making? After introducing themselves, I handed her a stack of books and told her she could go home and read them. Little did I know that was a sign of hope to her, that if she'd hang on and follow the teachings, God would deliver them.

Since then, David has become a man beloved by his wife, respected by his sons, trusted by his customers, honored by those in prison ministry with him, and has earned the admiration of his peers and leaders. For more than a decade now, the shelves of his basement which once housed pornographic video cassettes now contain video cassettes of the Gospel of Jesus Christ. His basement has been the site for more than one man he has led to a saving knowledge of Jesus Christ.

David is a man divinely transformed, not humanly reformed. There is an eternity of difference between the two. What God does is perfect and complete.

In this computer age it is possible to "boot up" a Bible program, put it in a window on the screen, then do the same with pornography off the Internet, and have the two side by side. The same can be done in the human mind. Men are living double lives today, trying to live for God, yet having their pornography too. The temptation to view porn in the privacy of office or home, with no one knowing, has caused it to become an addiction — and affliction — even to ministers.

I was in San Diego recently when two ministers' wives confided in me privately that their husbands were viewing pornography on the Internet. I realized this was just one more way that men could be stripped of their manhood, and lose what God had for them. Not having ever seen such things, I did what David's wife Barbara did recently and looked through what was offered when you "surf the net." I was shocked by the titles. Barbara rushed down to a computer store to find out how she could block that smut from coming into their home. Having no children to be concerned about, but my own consecration to God, I did something a little different.

After seeing the diabolical nature of what was offered, I put my computer on a table and placed a glass of non-alcoholic wine and an unleavened cracker in front of it. Sitting at the table before them, I made a covenant with God.

"This day I make a covenant with You, Lord. From this day forward this computer shall never have or show anything on it that is unclean, impure, or sinful."

I then took the wine and bread, elements of Holy Communion, Eucharist, the Lord's Supper. I consecrated myself in a covenant with God to keep myself pure from taint of sin through use of the computer. I did the same with the television, making a covenant and sharing in the Lord's Supper again.

Sitting there, having accomplished a most solemn act of worship, I realized something. For me to open up that computer and boot up pornography on it, I would have to cross the line where the elements were that I had used for communion. To do that, in essence, I would be forced to trample underfoot the blood and body of Jesus, as represented in the Christian sacrament.

In all good conscience I cannot now cross the line to the computer for anything unholy or profane. I have "sanctified" myself to the glory of Almighty God.

On a day after I told that to a group of men, a fine-looking young man approached me. "Sir, I went home last night and shared that with my wife. We knelt on either side of our bed and took communion. Also in front of our television we did the same. Then we found our marriage license and did the same with it on a table in front of us.

"It was so great! It was the first time I felt like a whole man. The Lord was so real to us. The Holy Spirit worked so powerfully in our lives. My wife and I seemed so pure, godly, and even holy. Last night had to be the greatest night of our marriage."

Having difficulty with pornography in your life? Are images in your mind holding you in bondage to an old life you detest?

Settle it!

Have the courage of your convictions to make covenant with God through Jesus Christ.

Take the sacrament our Lord gave us to celebrate our covenant with Him and establish yourself in faith. Don't make a truce with sin; win a victory.

He did it for you.

Now it's your turn!

P R I N C I P L E S *for* COURAGEOUS MANHOOD

◆ THE MOST POWERFUL THING YOU CAN DO IN LIFE IS CREATE AN IMAGE. THE NEXT MOST POWERFUL THING YOU CAN DO IS TO DESTROY AN IMAGE.

◆ TO CROSS THE LINE OF THE ELEMENTS FOR COMMUNION IS TO TRAMPLE UNDERFOOT THE BLOOD AND BODY OF JESUS.

◆ DON'T MAKE A TRUCE WITH SIN; WIN A VICTORY.

NINETEEN

JIM HALEK

COURAGE TO
GIVE

You gain by giving what you cannot buy with money.

Jim could hardly believe what he saw in the doorway of his hospital room. His minister friend, whom he expected to be hundreds of miles away, was coming toward his bed.

"How do you feel, Jim?" he asked.

"Pretty rough," Jim answered. "What are you doing here?"

"I'm here to pray for you," the man answered. Botchilism was slowly draining the life out of Jim, leaving him weak and the doctors worried. Already, several people had died because of eating the same cheese Jim had eaten, and many more were in critical condition.

"And this is?" his minister friend said, reaching to shake hands with a well-dressed visitor.

"My uncle, Mr. Simpson," Jim said. His uncle owned one of the nation's largest real estate firms. The minister shook his hand warmly, giving greetings, then said, "You're a member of the family, so you can help me pray. Come on, let's lay hands on Jim."

Jim could feel his uncle's hand tremble with uncertainty as he laid it on Jim's chest. The minister started praying, "Father,

I ask for the healing virtue of Jesus Christ to course through Jim's body. I rebuke death in Jesus' name, and the spirit of death that would try to destroy him, and I command this illness to come out of him. Father, I ask You to heal Jim and raise him up. In Jesus' name I pray, amen."

The minister opened his eyes, shook hands again with the uncle, patted Jim's shoulder, then turned and left the room. The uncle later claimed that he was a Christian, and he acted like the prayer was nothing unusual, although it was the first time Jim had ever seen him pray.

Later that night, Jim wondered about the brief visit. Doctors had told Jim and his wife Nellie that if Jim made it through the night, he had a good chance of recovery. He lay awake that night, praying to live, thinking of seeing his children grow up and some day having grandchildren to bless his home. The minister's words echoed through his mind repeatedly, and Jim prayed the same words out loud.

The next morning, the doctors pronounced him improved, upgraded his condition, and gave Nellie a good prognosis. Everyone Jim heard about who was infected by the botchilism-tainted cheese died except him. Dozens died. Jim survived.

Years later, on a bright April day, Jim sat in an airy hotel boardroom at a strategy meeting with that same minister. The man mentioned that no one had ever donated more than $20,000 to the ministry in a single gift. When Jim heard it, he instantly felt an impression deep in his heart. When he shared the incident and the amount he wanted to give with Nellie later, she agreed. They wanted to be the first to give the ministry a gift of $100,000.

Jim was a land developer who had left the world he knew to give his talent to the Lord in building churches. He and Nellie determined to go into the nonprofit sector and trust God for real estate deals to supplement their income. At one time he had earned millions, yet always remembered the time God had delivered him when his business left him $23 million in debt with $5 million of personal debt. He never declared bankruptcy, although it cost him his house and his pride. Through those difficult times, Jim had learned to put God first in every area and was happy now that God was first even in the use of his talents.

One of the lessons Jim had learned in giving was that he would receive from God based on his willingness to give to God. He learned that giving sacrificially, not out of his excess, would open the windows of heaven to him. He proved God by passing the test repeatedly. On several occasions he had given ministries checks for $10,000 when he didn't have the money and had to borrow, or empty every bank account to cover his check. But God had always provided. Now Jim and Nellie prayed that God would give them the $100,000 to make good on their heart's desire. In the back of their minds, they believed it would take at least a year.

But in three short months a land development opportunity came up that required some cash to put together. Jim did all the legwork, and a wealthy friend put up the cash. They never made a written agreement, but Jim knew that when his friend received the profits, which looked immediate, he would give Jim a good amount for Jim's work. By the time the deal closed, Jim was badly in need of money. He had taxes to pay, he needed cash flow in his business, and he had a conviction that he needed to pay off his house. But when he realized the deal was closing, he determined to pay his pledge first, and let God take care of the rest.

What Jim didn't know was that the minister friend was out of the country doing mission work, and funds for the ministry in the U.S. had completely dried up. It looked like the ministry would have to shut down when the man returned from his missions trip.

Jim and Nellie struggled with what they were to do. When Jim's friend called and told him he was on his way over to Jim's house, Jim wrote out a check for $100,000 and sent it via overnight mail to the ministry. But the friend never showed up. Jim and Nellie prayed. The next day the friend said he would come that night. Again he didn't show up. Jim called the ministry first thing the following morning to tell them not to deposit the check, but they had already deposited it and had written checks off it to relieve their financial situation.

Jim and Nellie continued to pray. That night, Jim's friend came over and handed him an envelope. When Jim and Nellie opened the envelope later, they saw a check for almost $400,000! Not only were they able to cover the check for their offering, but they were able to pay taxes and reinvest in their own business.

Writing that check to the ministry ranked as Jim's biggest test of faith, and since then his business has increased ten-fold, growing to $100,000,000 in contracts. Last year Jim and Nellie were able to give two-thirds of their income to Christian ministries. This year, as they faced a tax bill and other pressing needs, once again they emptied their checking accounts to give $20,000. Within a month, God blessed them with income many times over their offering, allowing them to make a substantial payment on their home, taking them one step closer to their dream of being entirely debt-free.

But stepping out in faith is not an easy habit to fall into. Often Jim awakes in the middle of the night, business dealings swirling through his mind and fear gripping him. He regularly cries out to God like he did that night in the hospital, asking God to show him how to build the churches, where to find good vendors, or how to make another land transaction to provide income. Each morning, he awakes with a new idea, a strategy, or a plan that is beyond anything he imagined the day before.

Puzzled and sleepless one night about how to put a theater-style sound system into a church, he cried out to God for help. He didn't want to spend the Lord's money on multiple engineering analyses, or worse, engineering mistakes. The next day in an elevator, he struck up a conversation with a man who turned out to be the executive vice president of an international audio business. They made everything from car stereos to theater sound systems. The man offered to design for free the system Jim described.

Another time, Jim walked into a room of hardened businessmen who had a stranglehold on the construction industry in the major city where Jim was building a large project. They were there to haggle over the contracts Jim had the power to award. And the way the building industry was set up in that city, they were Jim's only choices. As the men were standing around talking before the meeting, Jim saw a blind man in the corner with a Seeing Eye dog and walked over to greet him. For some reason he was moved in his heart and wanted to help the man.

"Can I pray for you?" Jim asked him.

"Yes, please do," the blind man answered with a faint smile. Jim laid hands on him and prayed for his healing and for him to know God.

"Thank you," the man said, patting Jim's hand. Then Jim left to take his seat for the meeting.

Raucous argument punctuated the lively meeting as the contractors squabbled over who would get Jim's business. Jim bargained hard, even though he had little clout or leverage. He sat back and watched them argue amongst themselves as he pondered how he could justify spending good church money on them. If his price was met, he'd feel right about it. But if not, he'd be throwing away the Lord's money on these carnal, angry men.

"Look," he said finally, interrupting their incessant arguments, "I just need the work done for the price I've quoted. Can someone here do it or not?"

The men exploded again into argument until a voice from the corner brought an immediate hush to the room.

"Give Jim what he wants," the voice said.

Jim looked at the blind man, still sitting in the corner, whom Jim had figured was only a minor player in the bargaining. As the man spoke, Jim saw that his was the voice of authority that every man in the room revered and followed. Again the man opened his mouth, and every eye riveted on his face.

"Just give Jim what he wants," he said. Then he leaned back and stroked the Seeing Eye dog lying by his side.

The powerful men in the room suddenly seemed too timid to break the silence. Jim waited and was astounded at what happened next. These overpriced, hard-nosed, hostile negotiators suddenly couldn't do enough to help each other out and ensure Jim's price was met.

One man spoke to another beside him, "Well, I guess I could share this contract with you, and we could do it for the price quoted."

Other men assented around the table, and the disparate group became unanimous in who would take which contracts. As they walked out slapping backs and laughing loudly with each other, Jim stayed behind to talk with his new friend.

"Thank you," he said to the man.

"Don't mention it," the man said. "But will you do me a favor?"

"Sure, anything," Jim said.

"Will you pray for my wife too? She needs it."

Jim agreed and they parted.

Jim says today that his gift makes room for him (see Proverbs 18:16), causes the Lord to rebuke the devourer for him, and opens the windows of heaven (see Malachi 3:10,11). He has the stories to prove it.

✠

Too often today people do too little for the Lord because they are uninspired. We hear testimonies of witnessing to others, going on missions trips, and other sacrifices, but we've made our fasting, prayer, and giving a secret, fearing that if we

197

discuss it, we'll become puffed up with pride. The concern is real, yet there is also a very real time and place to share humbly and allow yourself to be an inspiration to others. That's why I convinced Jim to allow me to tell you his story.

"You gain by giving what you cannot buy with money."

That precept is more than a mere aphorism or maxim. It is a principle upon which great blessings rest, and by which fortunes are made.

In His teaching concerning the kingdom of God and its principles, precepts, and laws, Jesus taught, *Greater love hath no man than this, that a man lay down his life for his friends* (John 15:13). Christ taught that you know the depth of love by the degree of giving.

The amount of a man's life given to his wife in marriage shows the depth of his love for her. The measure he keeps for himself reveals the shallowness of his love. How you give shows how you love.

Recorded in the Bible is the story of a man called Barnabas. When an offering was called for in the early church, he sold all his possessions and laid them at the apostles' feet. Later the Apostle Paul would write that those who gave a generous offering for his ministry had first given themselves to God. Their offering was determined by how much of themselves had first been given to God.

The love of Christ that Barnabas possessed, evidenced through his willingness to give to God's work, opened the door for him to become a missionary partner with Paul on his journeys. Barnabas became umbilically attached to the place where he put his money. So do we all.

Purity is best demonstrated by generosity. Jesus pointed this out in talking with the Pharisees. He rebuked them because they watched the external matters of their lives but neglected to care for the internal. Outwardly they were religious; inwardly they were ungodly.

Then Jesus said, *Woe to you, Pharisees, and you religious leaders – hypocrites! You are so careful to polish the outside of the cup, but the inside is foul with extortion and greed* (Matthew 23:25 TLB). It showed in their handling of money. God looks on the heart and sees the motive of our actions. (See 1 Samuel 16:7.)

Money gives value. How we use money shows the value system in our life. Some men would rather pay their wives alimony after divorce than give them money while they are married. Others think nothing of spending a small fortune on their hobby, but resent the price their wives pay for a new dress.

An offering to God shows respect and reverence for Him. What we give establishes His value to us.

The Apostle Paul apologized for not receiving an offering from the Corinthian believers. His failure to do so caused their lack of respect for him, even though he was trying to show his love for them by not being a burden to them.

Jim's desire to give the largest offering he had ever given, or the ministry had ever received, was not birthed in a selfish or greedy attitude. His heart and motive were pure. He wanted to honor God and show respect for the ministry that had changed his life. It was a noble enterprise.

God's respect for Jim's offering was shown in the outpouring of grace, work, and financial remuneration returned to him. Jim's gesture, rather than being a hindrance to others, became an incentive and challenge for others to do the same. He inspired other men and used a new level of commitment and faith he had never before known.

Jim's gift gained him greater love, appreciation, faith, friendships, respect, trust, honor, and favor — none of which you can buy with money. He used the intangible, abstract, invisible from which the tangible, concrete, and invisible are the result.

And as for those grandchildren he hoped to see one day, they are ever at his house playing and enjoying one of the youngest grandfathers I've ever known.

Jim has a deep reverence for God, a belief in His Word, a trust in His promises, and he exhibits it all by the investment of his life. His is a noble deed, worthy of recognition, gratitude, and honor. He represents all those who have been willing to underwrite the cause of Christ, support the Gospel with contributions, and invest themselves in His kingdom.

It takes courage to take such steps of faith. Jim has such courage. Because of it, a new level of life and a greater degree of manhood are attained. It enlarges and energizes the spirit. Inspires others to emulate great deeds. Challenges the pure, and censures the impure.

It was said of Barnabas that he was a good man, full of faith and the Holy Ghost. The same can be said of Jim.

God be praised if the same can be said of you.

P R I N C I P L E S *for* **COURAGEOUS MANHOOD**

♦   YOU GAIN BY GIVING WHAT YOU CANNOT BUY WITH MONEY.

♦   YOU KNOW THE DEPTH OF LOVE BY THE DEGREE OF GIVING.

♦   PURITY IS BEST DEMONSTRATED BY GENEROSITY.

TWENTY

LEIGH HOWARD-SMITH

COURAGE TO
KEEP A PROMISE

Your word is your bond.

When he saw her come up from the water, he looked at her face and knew she was in love with another man — and it wasn't him. "It challenged my manhood," Leigh said later.

Leigh and Denise had married when he was an executive with a trucking company. A few years after marrying, they drove his big BMW down the coast to have coffee at a quaint café in one of the little towns on the ocean, where Leigh told Denise once again his real dreams.

"I would love to have our own business," he said wistfully. "Something we could do in tandem with our skiing."

Upon returning to their spacious house in one of the most affluent neighborhoods in Sydney, Australia, Denise pondered what was at stake. Theirs was a good life of long ski weekends, theater, sports, and fun. As a connoisseur of fine wines, Leigh's cellar was stocked from floor to ceiling. His nightly ritual was choosing the right wine for dinner.

But when Denise agreed, Leigh resigned his plush corporate job at a company that became one of the largest transport businesses in the world. They sold their enormous house, and he launched out in quest of financial freedom and individual independence.

In two years Leigh was impoverished. His assets and holdings had all been invested and lost. Destitute, in debt, but still clinging to their will to succeed, they found an ancient garage on a seventeen-acre farm. Pipes ran on the floor. A sink sat in one corner. A charcoal barbecue for a stove forced them to eat outside so they would not have to breathe the smoke. Between them they worked six jobs, leaving at four in the morning and returning home at eleven at night. What little they had left after paying their debts, they saved.

Committed to a strict budget, Leigh's daily spending allowance was one dollar. Rather than spend it on lunch, he would save it to buy a bottle of cheap wine. Every evening he would stop at the same bottle shop for his one and only purchase. At night after dinner, he would sit under the night-time sky and enjoy his one and only respite from the rigors of the day.

As some shrewd money management and investing paid off, Leigh and Denise had a down payment for a comfortable new home in a modest community. With the difficulties behind them, they started a family. About that time, Leigh found a partner who wanted to start a new transport company. Together, they launched it.

When Leigh's new venture became profitable, they moved with their two small children back to a more affluent neighborhood. With the road to financial recovery in sight, they once again set about entertaining and enjoying some of the lifestyle they'd once known. One night at dinner, when Leigh brought out his best wines, it reminded his neighbor of a funny anecdote.

"When I owned the bottle shop," he said. "I worked evenings at this one store, and we had this idiot who came in every night to buy a ninety-eight cent bottle of wine. He was the only one who bought it, and we had to stock it just for him!"

Denise smiled as Leigh stretched across the table to shake hands with the man.

"Meet the idiot!" he said.

A neighbor in their new neighborhood witnessed to Denise about Christ, encouraging her with stories of a wonderful Savior Who would forgive her of all her mistakes and sins. Finally convinced, Denise gave herself completely to Christ. Her sudden joy was puzzling to Leigh. She could not stay away from church. Reading her Bible became a nightly ritual for her, as Leigh's wine was for him.

"Leigh, I want to ask you a favor," she said seriously one day. "Would you permit me to get water baptized?"

"You don't need that!" Leigh bellowed at her. "You've got enough without it!"

Denise walked away crestfallen, and before she could get out of the room, Leigh saw her joyful countenance turn to tears. An hour and a half later, Leigh could stand it no longer. Here was the woman who had endured all his foibles, who had stuck by him, and he couldn't even go with her one time to some dumb church to get baptized.

"If it means that much to you, you can and I'll go," said a penitent Leigh late that night.

Sitting in the back of the church, holding their children as a shield in front of him, Leigh watched Denise being baptized. When he saw the glow of love on her face for Someone other than him, it struck his heart as a blow and challenged his manhood.

Weeks later he heard about a men's event at the church on the subject of being a "real man." Leigh decided to find out what it was about. He went early that Saturday morning expecting to find a dozen or so men, but to his surprise over 700 filled the hall.

At the end of the first session, when the call was made to repent and believe on the Lord Jesus Christ, Leigh was the first to the front. He left the altar and walked out into the lobby of the building.

"Hello, Leigh," said a young man's voice. Leigh wheeled around him and saw four of his former employees from the transport company. He looked at them in disbelief. They had been incorrigible troublemakers.

"What are you doing here?" he asked. "I sacked you guys, and you're still talking to me?"

"God told us that one of our old bosses was going to become a Christian today," one explained.

"All week we've been wondering who," another said. "We never dreamed it could be you!"

While Leigh reacquainted himself with his former employees, one of the men at the church picked up a phone and called Denise.

"He what!" she exclaimed.

"He went forward for salvation," the man said again.

Denise waited with eager anticipation for Leigh to come home. A few hours later, she knew everything she needed to know when Leigh walked in and she saw the glow on his face that he'd seen on hers just weeks earlier.

Now with a new heart and a mind open to God's Word, Leigh grew in favor and in manhood. But at his company he saw troubling signs of something drastically wrong.

"What is it, Leigh?" Denise asked one night, when she saw his anxiety.

"Our profit and loss statement is way off kilter," he told her. "I've got to find out why."

"Let's pray," she encouraged.

Nights at home in prayer and days at work studying financial details began to reveal what was wrong. Leigh had to deal with it. The company was facing receivership.

"Your word is your bond" — the words he heard at men's meetings pounded in his mind. His reputation and company was being ruined by wrong decisions and his name was on the bottom line.

Vendors started demanding cash on delivery. Lawyers sapped him financially for their services while telling him, "File and forget it." Employee morale fell. Leigh's company was in chaos. He felt as though he was standing in the middle of a storm, being blown in all four directions at once. Should he try to salvage the company, or let it go?

One sleepless night, as he sought God for an answer, he read this passage: *Lord, who may go and find refuge and shelter in your tabernacle up on your holy hill? Anyone who leads a blameless life and is truly sincere. Anyone who refuses to slander others, does not listen to gossip, never harms his neighbor, speaks out against sin, criticizes those committing it, commends the faithful followers of the Lord, keeps a promise even if it ruins him, does not crush his debtors with high interest rates, and refuses to testify against the innocent despite the bribes offered him — such a man shall stand firm forever* (Psalm 15:1-5 TLB).

"Keeps a promise even if it ruins him." The words dropped immediately from his head to his heart, and he knew he would stay with the company and regain his good name. He had given his word to his partner, his employees, his clients, and his vendors. He would keep it, or die trying.

Leigh's partner agreed with him. Unified, the two faced charges, batteries of legal experts, government agents, vendors, all with nothing but the Word of God to stand on. Leigh had heard from God, and that's all he needed. God did not give Leigh the backbone for the job. God *was* Leigh's backbone.

The company had plummeted from twenty-four million in gross revenue to six million, and was teetering on the verge of being totally lost. Leigh and his partner worked night and day with agents, lawyers, bankers, and others. Denise helped them with all the paperwork. It was a trying time to go through, but the company slowly began to make a turn for the better.

Once the company stabilized, it began to gain back some of what it lost. At twelve million dollars in gross income today, Leigh is grateful for God's deliverance. But even greater, Leigh is grateful for what God has done within him in teaching him how to be a man of his word, a man of integrity with God and man.

Trust is limited to the extent of truth and no farther. Trust is back in Leigh's company today. Vendors, customers, employees, and bankers have learned to trust Leigh and his partner. It was hard to convince those who had suffered from before, but they gained confidence as they saw Leigh and his partner perform their promises.

God says that He watches over His Word to perform it. (See Jeremiah 1:12.) That is why He is known as our Redeemer. He redeems His Word. As men, we have to redeem our word as well. When we say we're going to do something, we have to do it. When Leigh was faced with an employee who said Leigh would do something, since the man was under Leigh's leadership, Leigh was bound to his promise.

One of the reasons many men live unfulfilled lives is that they have given their word and have not kept it. Men pile load upon load of guilt on themselves and then wonder what's wrong with them. It takes courage to give your word and keep it, but a man's reputation is only as good as his word, and his word is only as good as his character. Leigh's character was shown by his words, and soon everyone trusted in his company again — because they trusted his character.

It took courage for Leigh to go to church, courage to walk forward in front of those men to confess Christ. But if he'd not done it, he'd have never had the courage to keep his word in business and endure until he saw success.

It took living through a nightmare to make it possible for him to live his dream.

What God has done for Leigh, He will do for you! Become a man of God's Word — and a man of your word!

PRINCIPLES *for* COURAGEOUS MANHOOD

♦ YOUR WORD IS YOUR BOND.

♦ TRUST IS LIMITED TO THE DEGREE OF TRUTH AND NO FARTHER.

CONCLUSION

MEN OF
COURAGE

Time and space do not permit me to tell of every detail in the lives of the men in this book, nor to include others of equal stature, nor to describe the myriads of deeds done.

These are men such as Washington Ngede of Kenya, whose faith and courage is legendary in that nation. Or Roger Leyton in Central America, whose flame of passion for his countrymen burns brighter with the dawning of every day. Or Omar Cabrera in Argentina, who filled stadiums for those God said needed to hear and see the works of God.

I wish I could tell in detail of the seventeen-year-old young man who stood in front of the men's meeting and inspired them with his testimony. Dressed in shined black loafers, huge baggy pants with a chain drooping from belt to pocket, bandana tightly wound like a belt around his head, he spoke with a large Bible in his hand to illustrate his love for God.

"When I carried a knife nobody was afraid of me. I could ride with anybody anywhere. But since I began to carry this Bible, everyone is afraid of me. They won't come around me, let me ride in their cars, or spend time hanging around with me. They're afraid I'll talk about Jesus.

"I used to be afraid all the time. Afraid I'd get killed or busted. But I ain't afraid of nothing now."

The ballroom full of men stood, cheered, and applauded him, inspired by his courage and faith. There's George and Ruth Fitzgerald, who have come from divorce, drugs, prison, and poor parenting into the fullness of their ministry, with their two sons in ministry as well. Or I could tell of Keith and Peggy, who built a car hobby into a million-dollar truck stop business and are models of Christian virtue.

Then there's Lafayette Scales, the great pastor and minister to men. As a boy growing up in his neighborhood, he feared for his life walking down the streets. To protect himself he "bulked up" physically and learned to fight. Wearing a black "skull cap" and heavy beard, with a scowl to go with it, he looked intimidating. No one knew it was his way to deal with his fears.

In Singapore, telling men of those days, he brought them to their feet in applause, laughter, and appreciation, when he said, "If anyone challenged me, I would show him my fists. I held one up and said, 'This one is for the hospital,' and showed the other saying, 'and this one is for the cemetery! Which one do you want?'"

After three days of the most profound teaching any of us probably ever heard, the Bible school's students walked around saying, "This one is for the hospital, and this one is for the cemetery!"

These days LaFayette is busy keeping men away from both. Emulating Abraham, who took 318 men trained in his own household to rescue his nephew Lot, LaFayette has formed a group of men in his church called "The Three

Eighteen." They are men in covenant with God and each other who rescue brothers taken captive by the devil — a formidable force of faithful men filled with fortitude and faith.

Then there's Don. In so many men, money and faith go together. Rightfully so, since money is a visible fact of the work of faith. Money is sacred to God. It represents our lives. For giving our life at work we are given money in exchange. What we do with our money shows what we do with our life.

Don's first act of real faith in regard to money was the day the Spirit of God "led" him to give $300 to a pastor. It represented three months income for him, and food and shelter for his family. It was an immense amount of money at the time. He struggled with it for days, and finally put his wife in their car and drove to the city nearby where the pastor was living.

Unable to find the pastor, he inquired as to his whereabouts. A parishioner told Don, "When he came here he did it by faith, believing God sent him. Recently his debt became so large he decided he had to leave, find a job, and pay off his debts."

"How much were his debts?" Don asked.

"Three hundred dollars," she answered.

That lesson marked Don. It taught him to be responsive to the Holy Spirit, and that time is essential in life. It also taught him the need for patience to receive the promise, and how men lose the reward through impatience. It so marked Don, that after four decades, he still tells the story to illustrate his lesson in faith and courage.

It was Stephen, in Cincinnati, who said, "Money is not the most important thing in the world until you need it. Then it is!" After staving off bankruptcy for three long years and finally launching his new business, he said, "You don't drown by falling in the water. You drown by staying there!"

In every man, how he handles the pennies determines how he handles the millions. The only difference is a decimal point. It was Jesus Himself Who said, *No! For unless you are honest in small matters, you won't be in large ones. If you cheat even a little, you won't be honest with greater responsibilites* (Luke 16:10 TLB).

I can't even tell the great exploits of some of the most magnificent men I've ever met. It is endangering to the lives of the men in Uzbekistan, Nepal, and China to tell of what God is doing to reach the men in their nations with the truth, "Manhood and Christlikeness are synonymous!"

Hee Kong was a nineteen-year-old soldier when he heard that truth and made a determined choice to become a Christlike man. As the years went by, he held to his covenant resolution with God and started a church out of a home Bible study in his native Singapore. It was his choice, made in full realization of its meaning, to hold himself in faith and purity, both in spirit and body. His young converts refuse to worship their ancestors and come to church even today bloodied by parents angry with their denunciation of ancient religious tradition. Yet over 4,000 come every week and throughout the week, and most are under the age of twenty-five.

Under the influence of Kevin Dyson and following the example of Suliasi Kurulo's young men, Kong vowed he would not marry, nor even date a girl, for the first five years of ministry. Dr. Dyson walked into his office one day after a prayer meeting at home, and asked Kong if he ever thought about getting married.

"I vowed I wouldn't marry or even date for five years, and that time is up in just two weeks," Kong answered.

"Then think about it," Kevin said. "If you were going to marry, who would it be?" Kong pondered the question thoughtfully.

"Probably Sun," he finally decided. "She's been faithful in ministry. She's attractive. She's a woman of God."

"Then why not ask her," was Kevin's next question.

Pastor Kong walked into Sun's office, which was down the hallway from his, sat down, and asked her if she would consider marrying him. She laughed at first, then seeing his serious demeanor, she said, "What?"

"How about we talk to our parents, and in about thirty days, we get engaged?" Kong asked a second time.

"Okay," she answered.

But they were so self-conscious afterwards, they didn't speak again that day. Kong was so circumspect in behavior and careful before the other young people in the church, that only after they married did their real dating start. An exemplary man is making an exceptional minister.

On every continent, in every nation and city, there are men such as these, and their stories are continuing the book of Acts and the history of Jesus Christ. Jesus still works with men, confirming His message with signs following. No wonder all the books in the world would not be enough to tell the wonderful works of God. (See John 21:25.)

God never promises a good end to anything without providing the means to secure it. God promises heaven, and Jesus Christ is His means to secure our salvation, to make us acceptable for heaven. In every instance, the criterion for these men's lives was a love of the truth. The prophet Job said, *Just as my mouth can taste good food, so my mind tastes truth when I hear it* (Job 12:11 TLB). Truth is a moral and personal characteristic of God. The Word of God is the final and ultimate revelation and definition of God.

It is the Word which gives substance, the foundation of faith to stand and walk on. Men, nations, and earth itself can be shaken, but the Word never is. It holds both the promise and the means for every good end in life.

Franklin stated that when his life turned upside down with divorce, destruction of his business, and personal losses, the only constant in his life was God's Word. His glass of life wasn't half full or half empty, it was barren. One seed of truth planted in his heart and mind, with the tenacity bordering on obstinacy to hold on in faith, has produced a new life of fruitful abundance. Speaking to men around the world, he speaks from the authority of having "been there."

"I know God is able," he firmly states today. "I thought having absolutely nothing was the most devastating thing that could happen to a man. Now I realize it gave me the opportunity to build my life over again, and this time build on the Rock."

It was God's transcendent glory at work in his life, taking things meant for evil and making them work for his good.

Then there are men like Doug Stringer, whose courage and faith are capturing the attention of people around the world. His influence is being felt from the darkened streets of the city of Houston, Texas, to the offices of millionaires in Asia.

Turning his fitness center into a center for homeless and hopeless youth almost two decades ago, he has developed a pattern of ministry that is being effective on the streets of major cities on four continents. Typical of Doug is the incident that occurred between him and a caller to a radio program on which he was being interviewed. The interviewer asked him his belief about homosexuals.

"The Bible says it is a sin," was Doug's answer.

The next caller was a local leader of a national homosexual rights group who was out of a paying job because he was dying from AIDS.

"You're nothing but a religious bigot," the caller spat at Doug. "Your Christianity is a farce, your so-called care for people is nonexistent. You don't really love homosexuals. You're out to get us, you homophobic...."

"Let me ask you a question," Doug said, recognizing the caller whom he'd talked with many times before. "Does your organization believe in helping people? Do you care for each other?"

"Of course," the caller answered.

"Then who paid your electric bill last month when you couldn't pay it?"

"What do you know about that? What right do you have asking that?"

"Because our ministry paid it," Doug informed him. End of call. That Christian grace in action produced a deathbed salvation in the angry young man. Retelling the story of the man's salvation in a suburban church a year later, Doug brought a woman to tears. She told him after his message, "That was my son. Thank you."

Godly courage is revealed in more than one way.

Dale was sixteen when he made a quality decision. He wanted to remain a virgin until he married and not waste his youth dating and tempting himself with women. Dale was faithful to God's Word, and God was faithful to Dale. In prayer, God gave him a mental picture of the woman he would marry. He carried her image in his mind and heart.

Two years later as a senior in high school, while standing at his school locker, some freshman girls nearby were being capricious. In the clowning, one of them lost her balance and fell directly at his feet. When she looked up, he saw in her the reality of the picture God had given him. He courted her all through college, won her hand from her strict father, and married her seven years later.

As the pastor of a thriving church in Atlanta today, he proudly confesses to the glory of God they were both virgins when they married. He extols the blessedness of purity. It took the grace of God to bring them together, but it took good courage to maintain his virtue. It was the greatest gift he could give to her.

Richard gave a different gift. He and his best friend Mike were more than mere pals. They were 'buds,' closer than brothers, the kind who do everything together and stick close in every situation. But when Richard was converted to Christ, he had to tell Mike he could no longer do the illegal and illicit things they had engaged in before. Angry, Mike walked out of his life. It ruptured their relationship when they were just starting out in their early twenties. For twenty-five years Richard prayed for his friend, never knowing if he was dead or alive.

When the phone rang one afternoon, Richard recognized the voice immediately, though he had not heard it in two-and-a-half decades.

"Richard, the sheriff called me about all that trouble we used to be in," came the voice, "and I asked him if he knew if you were still alive. He gave me your number."

As they talked, Richard discovered that just six months earlier, Mike had made a commitment to Christ. The courage of his convictions twenty-five years before and faithful prayer in the intervening time brought unspeakable joy to Richard.

Some of these are simple deeds, others a lifetime choice, but they all speak of men who believed the truth and, by acting upon it courageously, gave evidence of their faith.

There are so many stories of so many courageous men, I could only tell you about a small fraction of those I know personally.

One thing they all did was to love truth, and when they acted on it in courage and faith, it sent them to a new level of life. That may be all that is keeping you from the level where God wants to take you.

Why settle for less when you can have more?

Take God at His Word. Be a man of courage.

EPILOGUE

We did not specify the ages of those we wrote of, for their ages span a half century, from those in their twenties to those in their seventies. The end of their stories has not and cannot be told, for they are still living. It will take their biographer at another time to tell the story of greater glory and exploits in Christ.

We also did not "factionalize," blending fact and fiction, except in a very few instances, to obscure those who may be hurt in the telling. Nor did we attempt to glorify these in any way, but rather to acknowledge deeds of which we have personal knowledge. There was no attempt to delve into attitudes nor emotions of which we knew nothing. Neither did we insert personal relational incidents beyond the necessary.

These men are compatriots in the faith whom we have associated with, prayed with, and worked with. Our admiration of them is clear and evident for overcoming heartache, obstacles, and personal faults and, through hurt and harm, for keeping the faith.

We have not hidden our affection for them as men whom we respect and even admire for their faith and courage.

May their lives bless yours even as they have blessed mine.

ENDNOTES

[1]Edwin Louis Cole, *The Potential Principle* (Springdale, PA: Whitaker House, 1984), 21.

[2]Edwin Louis Cole, *Maximized Manhood* (Springdale, PA: Whitaker House, 1982), 176.